Shaped by Fire

My Escape from Poverty's Pit

Shaped by Fire

My Escape from Poverty's Pit

Courtney R. Logan

Shaped by Fire: My Escape from Poverty's Pit

© 2014 by Courtney R. Logan

All rights reserved. No part of this work covered by the copyright herein may be reproduced, transmitted, stored, or used in any form or by any means graphic, electronic, or mechanical, including but not limited to photocopying, recording, scanning, digitizing, taping, web distribution, information networks, or information storage and retrieval systems, except as permitted under Section 107 or 108 of the 1976 United States Copyright Act, without the prior written permission of the Author or Publisher.

All trademarks are the property of their respective owners.

Published in association with Motion Publishing, LLC
Henderson, Nevada
www.motionpub.com

The author and publisher have made every effort to ensure the accuracy and completeness of information contained in this book at the time of press. However, we do not assume and hereby disclaim any liability to any party for any loss, damage, or disruption caused by errors, inaccuracies, inconsistencies, or omissions, whether such errors or omissions result from negligence, accident, or any other cause. Any slights of people, places, or organizations are unintentional.

Cover Photo: Mike Hume
Cover Design: Alvin Narag
Editor: Aja Williams
Interior Design: Chris Derick

ISBN: 978-0-9903796-0-7

Library of Congress Control Number: 2014908454

First Motion Publishing Edition: June 2014

*I dedicate this book to East St. Louis, Illinois.
Through your struggle beauty will be birthed into the Earth.*

CONTENTS

Foreword
Preface — xi
Acknowledgments — xiii
Introduction — xv
Chapter 1 - An All-American City Trashed — 1
Chapter 2 - Union for Greatness — 7
Chapter 3 - Safe Shelter — 15
Chapter 4 - My Refuge — 25
Chapter 5 - Brothers from Another Mother — 33
Chapter 6 - Alternate Path — 47
Chapter 7 - The Other Side of The Coin — 55
Chapter 8 - A New Beginning — 61
Chapter 9 - The Key — 71
Chapter 10 - The College Experience — 81
Chapter 11 - The Little Girl Around the Corner — 89
Chapter 12 - Road to Love—Through Love — 97
Chapter 13 - Taking the Legal Road — 105
Chapter 14 - Creative Policy — 113
Chapter 15 - A New Direction — 129
References — 135
About the Author — 137
How to Help This Book — 139

FOREWORD

It is my great pleasure to have the privilege to write this foreword for my grandson, Courtney R. Logan.

As described in the text of the book, Courtney came to me as a very small child due to unfortunate family circumstances. Courtney has always been a peculiar child. He has always searched for answers and taken the bold approach to life.

I am godly proud of Courtney for his accomplishments, despite his situations, or perhaps because of his situations. Courtney has always had an attitude of prevalence about him. Instead of being bitter about his situation, he allowed those same circumstances to make him better. He has always been determined to pull himself up from the life he was born into and make a better life for his family and himself.

He has that same determination to bring others along with him by letting them know that your circumstances do not control your destiny—only you and God are the masters of that journey. This is a book about poverty, drugs, and perhaps poor parenting—but that is not the essence of the story. This story's essence is triumph and victory over those barriers.

— Ernestine Price

Preface

How *did you do it?* This is the primary question that helped spawn this book. Typically, after I describe my background and life to people, the first thing they would like to know is "How?" How does a person from a combination of unfortunate circumstances make it to where you are today? But for me, the most important question has always been "Who?" And to answer that question I began to write these pages. I wanted an opportunity to share my perspective on growing up in East St. Louis, Illinois, to those who may be trapped in a similar environment. It is critical that young kids know there are exits embedded in their situations. More importantly, they need a first-hand account from someone who has stood in their shoes and walked their path.

Also, my unique experience growing up in the inner city and attending public school for my primary education can help equip policymakers. I will give them an inside perspective into what programs are effective and those that need to be improved. Hopefully, in turn I can help decrease the education gap between the inner city and suburban America. Far too many times people want to give assistance, but they lack first-hand knowledge, insight, or experience in order to implement or facilitate the right programs. Furthermore, in order to be effective policymakers, teachers, and school administrators they must know or have an idea of what goes on in a child's life when the school bell rings and children go home. This book is a glimpse into that world.

Writing this book was a very tough process. There were many nights I thought my time would be better used in other areas of my life. However, with each page I wrote the more I understood that withholding my story would be selfish. Thus, I labored nights and weekends for many months in order to finish this book. I wanted the painstaking writing process to be over. Early on, I tried to publish this book twice before it was actually ready, but my editors stopped me. It was clear that I was rushing. Instead, I took the time to craft and re-craft my life's story to ensure it is as powerful on paper as what I lived.

I wanted to ensure this book felt realistic. I wrote it speaking directly to you as if you were one of my closest friends. You will see there is not any back-and-forth dialogue, but instead me telling you my life's what, when, where, why, and how. Unfortunately, I will never have the opportunity to personally thank or speak to each person that reads this book, but in some way I hope that the words contained on these pages add value to your life. Thank you.

Acknowledgments

This book would not have been possible without the unwavering support of my wife, Rachel Logan. I am grateful for the many hours you allowed me to be absent from your presence so I could pour my heart and soul onto these pages. Thank you for your unconditional love and always reminding me of the destiny God has placed in front of me.

To my family, I am nothing without your love and encouragement. You have never turned your backs on me, and I am honored to be in the family I was born into. Many hearts and lives will be changed by our story.

To my friends, I am blessed to have you at my side. You continue to put your blind faith in me even at times when the path does not seem bright. I am truly blessed to be surrounded by great people.

To my mentors, thank you for believing in me. Your time and efforts continue to help me craft my present and future. Thank you for continuing to broaden my vision, and accept nothing but excellence.

To Wid, Krista, Jeremy, and Aja, thank you for helping me throughout the book writing process with your expertise, advice, and insight. Whenever I got stuck one of you was there to plow me out and give assistance. Thank you for being patient with me during this process.

To Mike, Alvin, Chris, and Ces, I greatly appreciate all of your help with design, graphics, and photography. Thank you for using your talents to help me bring this book to life.

To Phil and Motion Publishing, thanks for enabling me to publish this book.

To all of you who have donated, reviewed, and helped to develop this book, I am grateful.

To my daughter Courtney Robin Logan: I hope I have made you proud.

Introduction

I should be already dead. By day, I was consumed with the normal worries of being a black boy living in the hood. By night, the echoes of 9-millimeters and 12-gauge shotguns rocked me to sleep. I grew up with front-row seats to an ugly but fascinating underworld of poverty, drugs, and violence. My childhood was stripped from me. My family was in turmoil. My future, according to the statistics, was bleak. By the time I was a teenager, I had lived more than a 40-year-old man could attest to.

I've been making the same choices every day of my life: Not to become another sad statistic but rather strive to be someone my family is proud of, a person of integrity, a successful man in every sense of the word. This was not always a simple task. Many people never knew the demons I fought growing up because I was able to mask it so well. I made the choice when I was younger that I did not want other people's sympathy for my hardships, but instead I chose to endure. These choices have built my unconquerable character.

However, the fact remained that as much as I tried, I was not immune to the environment in which I lived. Loneliness was my shoulder to cry on in my time of need, and poverty raised me. But luckily for me, the bullets missed me, alcohol and drug addiction were not inherited by me, and blood money from drug dealing did not attract me. In fact, I am now a lawyer licensed to practice law in two states. I am an associate attorney at a defense law firm, Special Assistant State's Attorney in St. Clair County, Illinois, and Assistant Adjunct Professor of Law at St. Louis University School of Law. So now, it remains a mystery of why I am still alive that I write this book.

This book is an exit sign to those who might be trapped in the nightmare I relived daily as a young child. It is a guiding light to a path of success that can be obtained if you refuse to quit. More importantly, embedded in my story is a hope injection for your darkest hour. Just one single thread of hope can unlock doors you never imagine existed. It has for me. In this book, I will share the unfiltered truth about the process it took for me to become the man I am today. I want to give you an all-access pass to my past, and peel back the layers of achievements in order for you to see the true pain and suffering I had to endure. Then, you can have a better understanding that wherever you are in your life you too can obtain greatness and success.

In all actuality, I am just an average guy, but I have extraordinary vision. At a young age, I felt I was destined for greatness, but I also knew it would take work. Work that could only be performed by me, and I knew there was a long road ahead. There were many times I wanted to throw in the towel and give up. The uncertainty if I would ever make it out of the hood kept me second-guessing whether my future was as bright as I thought. I remember always feeling, "What does a person do when the right doors are always locked?" However, I never let this fear overtake me. You can't either. It is perfectly fine to have these feelings or questions. It is only human to feel these things growing up in such a brutal environment. On the other hand, you cannot let these thoughts determine your future.

As I retrace my life's story one phrase comes to mind: "refuse to be denied." My focus remained on my goals regardless of the things going on around me. Some would call it luck, and others would call it favor. Whatever verbiage you choose to describe it, there is no denying the simple fact that many who have walked my path never have the opportunity to share it. Now I tell my story boldly. In total disregard from what I was taught. Where I am from people do not believe in calling the cops because we lived by street law. What's more, we never tell family business.

Fundamentally, I see this as part of the problem. In this book, I will show you the pitfalls I saw all around me so you can avoid or strategically handle them. I will break the silence so that you will be able to make informed decisions about your future. I will take you behind the curtain of my family so you have the opportunity to save yours. I will show you how I stood toe-to-toe with poverty—and won!

It has been said that we are all products of our environment, victims of our circumstances. No rational person could deny the fact that where you are born and who your parents are heavily influence what you will become. I was conceived and born into chaos. However, it is also true that God created all of us with free will. He gave us minds and hearts that are capable of embracing hope and goodness. I believe... no, I know from personal experiences that we can overcome any challenge we face and rise above any adversity.

My family is everything to me. I love my grandparents, parents, siblings, aunts, uncles, and cousins dearly. Many of these people made the wrong choices in life; some of them still are making the wrong choices. But I have learned that, while it may not fit neatly into the cliché of "conventional wisdom," even people who make wrong choices can still be good people. By "good people" I mean folks who love and care about their own, who do everything they can to help those they love.

It's so easy to judge but much harder to love.

I learned about love from my grandmother, Ernestine Price, when she rescued me from foster care. I learned about love from Beverly Price, my father's wife. Although she's not my biological mother, she took me in and treated me as one of her own. I learned about love from my father, Robert Lee Price, Jr., who worked two jobs all of his life to make sure that his kids had food on the table.

I learned about love in East St. Louis, Illinois.

East St. Louis is a place that most Americans would like to forget about, to sweep under the rug, to pretend does not exist. Politicians have largely ignored or exploited my city. It's a criminal's playground. East St. Louis has one of the highest rates of violent crime in America. Its legitimate economy is in shambles. But for me, it is home. I love East St. Louis, but I don't deny that some label it with the unfortunate status of America's "war zone."

In 1986, I was born into a city that was in great distress and, sadly, it remains in great distress today. But there is light in my hometown, along with the darkness. That's my story, how by the grace of God and with the support of my family, friends, and community, I rose above the hate, the crime, the violence, the substance abuse, and the poverty. I rose above all of that evil and became not only a practicing attorney, but a whole and healthy and blessed human being. Regardless of what you are facing in your life, present or past, you can also rise above the adversity.

CHAPTER 1

AN ALL-AMERICAN CITY TRASHED

In order to tell you about my life, I first must share with you the history of East St. Louis.

My community is a place that has been cursed by a vicious combination of tragic circumstances, deliberate neglect and corruption. The acclaimed author Jonathan Kozol wrote about my hometown in his book, Savage Inequalities. Kozol's book, one of many he has written on the subject of racism and poverty in America, was published in 1991 and describes the East St. Louis of the late 1980s.

If you live in East St. Louis or in the Midwest, what I'm about to share with you will come as no surprise. However, if you don't and you're blessed to live in one of the vast majority of cities in our great country that are free from the curses of urban blight, environmental contamination, and economic deprivation, then prepare to be shocked by these facts that Kozol reported:

The East St. Louis I was born into was—and still

is—98% African American. In 1986, nearly one-third of the families in East St. Louis lived on $7,500 per year or less; 75% of the population was on public assistance. The U.S. Department of Housing and Urban Development described East St. Louis then as "the most distressed small city in America." A professor at the University of Southern Illinois said my hometown was "a repository for a non-white population that is now regarded as expendable."

From 1977 to 1989, the city was forced to lay off 1,170 of its 1,400 employees. The mayor said that he might need to sell City Hall and the fire stations in order to raise the cash required to meet operating expenses. Trash collection ceased in October 1987. Uncollected waste was feeding rats as "big as puppies," "bull rats" as the residents called them. The smell of burning garbage was prevalent daily. By 1989, raw sewage was backing up in the homes of residents in Villa Griffin, a public housing project. Raw sewage was also flooding basements and even public schools all over the city. The infrastructure of East St. Louis was crumbling, and there was no money or municipal employees available to fix the mounting problems.

Soil samples tested at residential sites in East St. Louis turned up disturbing quantities of arsenic, mercury, and lead as well as steroids dumped throughout the years by stockyards in the area. The air above the city was a brownish yellow from toxic smoke vented from the Monsanto plant's massive 400-foot-high smokestacks. Dead Creek, a creek bed that received discharges from chemical and metal plants through the years, was a place where East St. Louis kids rode their bikes. The creek smoked by day and glowed on moonless nights. It gained notoriety throughout the years for instances of spontaneous combustion. The Illinois EPA believed that the combustion started due to children riding their bikes across the creek bed, which "created friction which began the smoldering process."

East St. Louis had some of the sickest children in America in the 1980s. Of the 66 cities in Illinois, East St. Louis ranked first in terms of fetal death, first in premature birth, and third in infant death. There was no place to have a baby in East St. Louis; the maternity ward at the city's Catholic hospital was closed years earlier. Health care services of all types were extremely limited.

Death by homicide was also a real risk for an East St. Louis resident. Cities in Illinois of roughly the same size as East St. Louis in the '80s had an average of four homicides per year, but there were 54 murders per year in East St. Louis. State troopers were routinely sent into the city to put out disturbances that the police could not control. Crime rates were off the charts. The bleak pattern was repeated all too often—young black men with no education and no jobs turned to drug dealing to make money and ended up in prison or in the morgue.

In the late 1980s, unemployment reached 21% and that number grossly understated the true rate of joblessness because it did not account for people who had simply given up trying to find a job. In 1969, the tax base for the city was

$164 million; by the late 1980s, the tax base had dropped to less than $30 million. In the 1960s, East St. Louis was a prosperous and racially diverse community of 85,000 residents and had been named an "All-American City." By the 1980s, the population had dropped to 30,000 and East St. Louis was described as a "Third World city dropped into America's heartland." This was due to the industry leaving the area, and the death of the railroad for better roads and bridges. So the jobs left. Then those people who could afford to leave left. What was left? A heavily populated community of blacks and a few poor whites.

Have things improved in East St. Louis over the past three decades? On the whole, sadly not. The same awful cycle seems to be repeating itself, day after day, month after month, year after year.

But all is not lost.

In the midst of all this sadness and oppression, many people rise up, take control of their lives and prosper. I grew up, went to college and law school and got married. While some of my friends and family are in prison or dead, some of my friends and family are alive and happy and free. Some are rising up to become leaders in their industries and communities.

What makes the difference? What tips the scales? What compels one man to do anything and everything he can to triumph over his environment where another man just gives up, succumbs to the darkness, and becomes another log in the sad pile of humanity that makes up the most desperate parts of our nation?

By telling you my story, I want to help make a difference. I want you to make wise choices and decisions. Journey through these pages with me on the path to truth using my life as a roadmap. Some people might not like the truth because it does not neatly fit into the boxes we create to rationalize our lives, to justify our prejudices, or to explain away why we are not the people we truly want to be. My life does not fit in a box.

As it has been said, "The truth shall set you free."

If I have learned anything in my short life it is this—the truth will not be denied. You can run, you can hide, but, sooner rather than later the truth catches up with you. Here is my truth.

CHAPTER 2

UNION FOR GREATNESS

When I was born in 1986, my parents, Robert L. Price, Jr. and Pansy Logan, lived together. They struggled at that time, each in their own way, with the consequences of their poor choices and challenging circumstances.

My family is not a sitcom; we are not those portrayed on "The Cosby Show." My parents faced serious challenges; struggles they shared with many others in my poverty-stricken community. The heart of my family's issues lies in two words—substance abuse.

Although I have no hatred or disdain in my heart for people who abuse drugs or alcohol, I have learned in the hardest way possible that drug dealing and substance abuse, in a socio-economically depressed city such as East St. Louis, is both the spark and gasoline that ignites the flames that destroy lives and devastate communities.

In no way is my story an attempt to be judgmental and say, "You are a bad person, you did bad things." On the contrary, this is a story of hope and triumph, of faith and love. But as I said, the truth has a way of presenting itself, and it cannot be denied.

As an adult and serving in the role as a Special Assistant State's Attorney for the State of Illinois, I've learned that life is not always black and white, and people's actions are not as easy to categorize as absolutely right or absolutely wrong. This means we must journey into the uncomfortable gray areas in order to lift people up, and not tear them down from a distance sitting on our hands.

What I will share might seem out of the ordinary. For me nothing about my family life seemed odd. As a child, it was all I knew. I was a kid tossed into the middle of a whirlwind. As an adult, married with my own daughter, I can appreciate the unusual nature of my parents' relationship. I can see both the beauty and the hardship created by my father's decision to live with one woman while remaining married to another. I grew to accept it, but it was not a model that I wanted to emulate when I got older.

My father chose to live life on his own terms. In some ways, he felt life had broken so many rules that he did not want to play by the book either. He had a rocky childhood himself with a father who enjoyed alcohol. Looking back, he did things the way he did it and while I would certainly not want to emulate his lifestyle, I understand and empathize with his actions.

Growing up, there were many times I wished Dad worked a more prestigious job and that we lived in a house with a picket fence in a subdivision. If that happened, maybe then he would be able to spend more time with me and help me grow as a young man. But this was not the hand I was dealt, so I pressed forward. He loved me the only way he knew how and probably the way his father loved him. Despite everything, my father was and remains my hero.

Dad was born in 1950 and grew up in East St. Louis. His father, Robert Price, Sr., was an Alderman for Golden Garden, which is a smaller township of Centreville, Illinois. He was a well-known local political figure. He championed the people he represented. More importantly, he championed his family. My grandfather set the foundation for all the men in my family. He often told me, "In order to be successful in the world, you must first respect yourself and then respect others."

"Back in the day," as Dad puts it, jobs were plentiful in our city. The African-American population was largely confined to the city proper, but the surrounding area was racially diverse and quite prosperous. When my father was growing up, the city began its steady decline.

Dad missed out on many good things in life. He too was a victim of circumstances. He was an outstanding athlete, playing football and basketball in high school. Although he was a bit undersized, he excelled and was full of potential.

A silly, minor dispute with his coach ended his athletic career. Looking back, that was truly a shame. A few words from a person that could have offered encouragement rather than condemnation altered my father's entire future.

My father was talented enough that he could have earned a football scholarship to go to college. This may have kept him out of Vietnam and exposed him to ideas and people that would have molded his character in a different way. However, college was not in the cards for him, but war was on the horizon.

After high school, Dad worked for a time at Granite City Steel in Granite City, Illinois. He married his wife, Beverly Price, and stepped in as a father to my two older brothers, Paul and Chris Price, who she had prior to their relationship. Nevertheless, they were and are Dad's children. Shortly thereafter he was drafted into the service and left for Vietnam in 1971.

Dad was a Fighting Engineer in the U.S. Army between 1971 and 1972. According to my father, Vietnam was "a decent trip," and he "learned a lot of things." Although he might have learned some valuable skills and acquired some good qualities, overall he came back a different man—less trusting, more cautious, and definitely more attuned to the social changes happening around him. He was never the same as he was before the war. After his return, he became, in his words, a "wild boy" and began to live in "Crazyville."

There is no doubt in my mind that Vietnam changed my dad for the worse. My mother believes that my father suffered from Post-Traumatic Stress Disorder (PTSD) and that this condition was a serious negative factor in his life long after he returned home from the war.

Before he left for Southeast Asia, my father did not

have a drinking problem, but when he returned, he began a two decade-plus slide into alcoholism. Seagram's Gin was his drink of choice. In his words, he "loved gin but gin did not love him." He explained that gin effectively turned him into a real-life "Dr. Jekyll and Mr. Hyde." He began to drink a fifth of gin or more every day—it was a ritualistic habit he would continue until 1997 when he quit drinking for good.

Despite his issue with gin, my father was a hard worker. He went to trade school and became a truck driver. He later learned how to lay bricks. Eventually, he went to another school and was taught how to repair diesel engines. He became a diesel mechanic at Bi-State Development Agency, our local public transportation company, where he worked for 18 years. He also worked for many years at Midwest Rubber Plant.

My father taught me many things when he was sober, but perhaps the most valuable was if you want something in life, you have to work for it. By his example, I learned the virtues of diligence and persistence. More importantly, I learned selflessness. Dad would give you the shirt off his back if you needed it. Although he had a tough outer shell, I was able to discern his love and compassion for his family and friends through his continuous sacrifices. Those attributes were contagious.

I recalled my father being there to aid me whenever I was in distress. I remember being stranded on the side of the highway, and before I hung up the phone, he was half way to my location. I used to tell my friends, "I'm never too far away that my dad cannot get to me." It was in part my mantra growing up. I knew that my father would bring his life to a halt for a relative or a friend. Although he probably does not know it, he is the reason many people consider me a great friend. I acquired this sense of prioritization for people that are close to me. My father gets all the credit for that.

About 30 years ago, around 1983 or so, my father met my mother, Pansy Logan. Mom had been estranged from her husband for quite some time, but they never divorced. Dad fell in love with her quickly and still loves her passionately to this day. Dad did not divorce Beverly and marry my mom. By the time my parents met and fell in love, my father's relationship with Beverly had changed. Although they still liked each other and loved each other like family, they were no longer living as husband and wife.

So Dad simply moved on with his life, but I never really knew why they did not divorce at that time. My dad and mom moved in together, a home they still live in now, and for many years, he bore the expenses of keeping up two households—the one he shared with my mom as well as Beverly's. None of this was kept secret from anyone.

My mother, like my dad, had a serious substance abuse problem. In Mom's case, her demon wasn't alcohol, it was crack cocaine.

As a child, I hated crack. I always wished that my mother would shake her addiction to it. I never understood how she could love something so much that she put it before me. In my mind, crack was the sole reason I felt like a motherless child searching for nurturing arms to hold me. Homemade crack pipes were the reason I had to claim other people's moms as my "play mother." While it may have been cute for some of those women to "adopt me," it was a very real void I was trying to fill. Mothers have a unique role in a child's life of imparting love and care. Unfortunately, I was forced to look elsewhere for these qualities because my Mom was a drug addict.

Pansy is 12 years younger than my father. She grew up in a large family with seven children in Madison, Illinois, which is a small town close to East St. Louis. By 1975, as a young teen, my mother started using drugs. She also got caught up, in her words, in the whole "racial and gang thing." When crack cocaine became widely available in the early 1980s, my mother tried it and was instantly hooked. She remained a slave to this evil menace until very recently. Thankfully, she is now sober just like my dad.

I am the child of two serious substance abusers. Some would say I might be predisposed to become a substance abuser myself. Thankfully, I have never had those problems. That's a miracle.

That's also a choice.

From the outside looking in, it is easy and tempting to say that my parents were weak, selfish people who often put their own desires and issues ahead of their children's welfare. There is no denying the fact that my parents had problems, but they also had virtues. Most of all they loved each other. Despite mistakes that would destroy most relationships, they have stayed together through it all.

The reason they succeeded as a couple is because at their core they are both great people. When my mom was around, she would not only protect me from my father when he was caught up in his madness, she also did everything in her power, even though it was limited, to ensure I had the opportunities to be a kid. She planned birthday parties and convinced my dad that it was OK for me to go play in the neighborhood. When she was around, she was my advocate.

My mom has always been a woman of faith. She would tell you that it has been an unbelievably difficult struggle for her to overcome her raging addiction problem. She blames no one but herself for her substance abuse. Her nearly uncontrollable desire to get high cost her dearly. In many ways, she will pay the price for her poor choices for the rest of her life. I can finally say, after all this time, I am proud of the woman she has become. I am happy I lived long enough to witness her transition first-hand.

Dad also suffered, but by the grace of God, he was able to pull himself out of the bottle cold turkey and on his own accord. He would also tell you that there is no one to blame for his troubles but him.

Yet my parents endured. I endured and indeed prospered. Through faith, we have all come a long way. Through faith, we will travel the rest of our journey together.

CHAPTER 3
SAFE SHELTER

In the fall of 1990, the State of Illinois had to step in because my parents could simply no longer care for us. I was 4, my sister Crystle Price was 3. My little brother Robert C. Price (Baby Robert) had just been born.

Crystle, Baby Robert, and I became wards of the state. I was scared and lonely. I felt abandoned, hurt, and confused. I did not comprehend or fully grasp what was happening. We were stripped from our parents and shuttled between a few foster homes and eventually found ourselves in the care of a small group of Catholic nuns who operated a home for foster kids with nowhere else to go.

I don't remember much about the other foster homes where Crystle, Robert, and I were sent, but we were shuffled around separately to different homes. Back in the early 1990s, St. Augustine of Hippo Catholic Church operated a small facility on its Columbia Place property dedicated to the care of foster kids such as us. It was not a permanent home but rather a place of refuge; somewhere children could be sent and cared for until family came to retrieve them or the state could assign them to long-term foster care.

I have bittersweet memories of Sister Jean and Sister Carmen, the two nuns who ran the foster home. The Catholic Church has been a presence in East St. Louis since the founding of the city in the 19th century. St. Augustine of Hippo Catholic Church remains on Columbia Place and continues to be an active parish today.

The nuns did their best to give us a sense of normal life and a caring environment. I remember them taking us to the circus and other events. They ensured we had food and had proper hygiene. At all times, they made sure that we were properly looked after and in good hands. They were great, but the situation that got us there was very ugly.

I remember my father coming to visit at Christmas that year. He brought me a little red fire truck. However, the toy did not make up for the somber emotions I felt when his visit time ended. Every time he walked out of the door, I remember feeling unloved and worthless. In utter disappointment, I remember thinking to myself, "Does he really love us?" I can still feel the door closing on Christmas Day. Unfortunately, I had many of those little red fire truck moments as a child.

I don't recall exactly how long we lived with the nuns on Columbia Place, but it was several months. It seemed like forever. Can you imagine being separated from everything you know and love? That place never felt like home, instead if felt like a children's prison. This isolation explains why children in foster care are nearly two-and-a-half times more likely to seriously consider suicide and four times more likely to have attempted suicide than other youth. While we were there, my family worked as hard as they could to get us out of state care and back into a family member's home.

As has been the case all of my life, my extended family was always nearby and willing to step in and help. The state was about to put us up for adoption, and there was a great possibility that we would be separated. But we were soon rescued by my grandmother.

My father could not get legal custody of us on his own, so he asked his mother, Ernestine Price, who was 63 years old at the time, to get us out of foster care. Against the opposition of other family members, she became my legal guardian when I was 5 or 6. Some relatives felt that my grandmother was too old to be taking on three younger children. Besides, she had already raised her own kids and had a full career. She retrieved my sister, brother, and me from the Catholic home for displaced kids.

The night my Grandma Price picked us up from foster care, she had a discussion with my sister Crystle and me in the back room of her home. The first thing she explained to us was that we were to always be respectful to adults. She talked to us about the virtues of good manners, and shared with us her expectations in her home. I learned the key phrases "ma'am" and "sir" that night. Thinking back, I cannot imagine the pressures she had going on in her life being newly retired and taking on so much more responsibility. This is a person that picked 300 pounds of cotton per day when she was younger, retired from the education field, raised her own family, and now she was taking us in her home. She did all this with a smile and made it look seamless.

Thank God for grandmothers.

I lived in her house, off and on, for many years until I graduated from high school. Words alone cannot express the love and admiration I have for Grandma Price. She provided me with a sense of love and security at times when I had nowhere else to turn. She taught me life skills that would later allow me to be self-sufficient.

Grandma Price lived on Jefferson Road, in Golden Garden. Grandma's house was an incubator of solid character. While I was in her home, she shielded me from substance abuse and criminal activity that ran rampant around me. When my father would be engaged in his drunken escapades, my grandmother was the only person who could reach him. Generally, people knew that my grandmother would not tolerate disrespecting her or her home. This included my dad and anyone else that would make her house unsafe. While she is the smallest person in my family, she has the heart of the fiercest lion.

During this time, Ernestine and Robert Price, Sr., my grandparents, owned a small tavern-type establishment that had games and pool tables. My older brothers and cousins frequented this place. I have fond memories of being a pest under their feet as they tripped over me trying to play pool or socialize. My grandfather had a milk crate for me to stand on to play the Ms. Pac-Man machine—with his quarters, of course. There were some not-so-great memories at the pool hall as well. One night, my parents bought some fish, and I asked for some. My mom told me that it had lots of bones inside so be careful. During my first bite of the fish, a bone got stuck in between my top and bottom teeth. My mouth was stuck open. We drove to my grandparents' pool hall, where my dad went to work with some wire pliers. Eventually, the bone was removed, and that was my last bite of fish—for that night at least.

By the time I entered second grade, I lived mostly with my father, but I moved back and forth between his house and Grandma Price's. Dad's house is just south of St. Clair Avenue near Church Lane on 79th Street. My definition of home, unlike many people's, was not limited to one physical location. Sometimes home would be Grandma Price's and sometimes it would be Beverly's. I lived the true definition of "home is where the heart is." Many times school felt like home.

From my father's house, I could walk to school, Warren G. Harding Elementary. Almost all of my childhood friends lived in Dad's immediate neighborhood, other than the ones I met while staying with my Grandma Price. Growing up, I was primarily relegated to 98% black neighborhoods and was not exposed to other races of people.

My close friends and family would tell you that I've

never met a stranger. I have a genuine love for people—whether they are black, white, or brown, it matters not to me. I'm a great talker, but a better listener. I'm an extrovert for sure. I'm the guy who makes friends in the airport at 3 a.m. waiting for a red-eye flight.

As an adult, I have been exposed to a variety of cultures and subcultures. One of the things that strikes me as being very different about the community I grew up in versus a "typical" American suburban upbringing (regardless of race) is the definition of family.

Most children look for love and support primarily to their parents, and, to a lesser extent, their grandparents. That comprises the essence of "core family." I considered my core family to be my parents, grandparents, uncles, aunts, and cousins. This broader definition of core family (not extended family) is not unique to the African-American community, but with us it takes on a special flavor.

East St. Louis was, and remains, a very harsh environment. The people who live there largely survive like my family survived, by pooling their resources and helping each other.

When I needed anything growing up—from a new pair of shoes, to clothes, a ride to ball practice, or a helping hand in any way—many arms were outstretched to me, not just a couple of sets. This is normal to me. It's how I am today.

For instance, my next-door neighbor would always open his wallet to give me bus fare if I needed it. My Aunt

Brenda regularly paid bills at my father's house in order for us to have basic necessities such as electricity and water. School teachers would buy me lunch on field trips when I did not have the money. My close friends would share their money with me when we went to the corner store. The list of blessings I received was endless, and the way I repaid them was by staying out of trouble.

My father had a wonderful habit; he made sure that no one ever left his house hungry. If you came for a visit, you ate something regardless of what time of day it was or who you were. It's the little kindnesses like that I remember, and it is that kindness that I have incorporated into my everyday life.

Through a combination of ingenuity, sacrifice, and sheer determination, people in East St. Louis survive in what can only be described as brutal circumstances. From personal experience, I can tell you that the notion that African-American people are lazy and do not want to work is a myth. Worse, it's an ugly lie. It is a lie used by people with bad intentions to justify the social policies that keep communities such as East St. Louis down.

Some of the most frequently asked questions by people who are not from my hometown, people I have come in contact with through my career or when I was on the college debate team, are "How did you survive growing up?" or "You are so articulate" and "You seem so 'normal,' Courtney, you are such a nice guy, how did that happen?"

While I understand there may be good intentions

behind some of these comments, there are some embedded harmful assumptions. Is an African-American man not supposed to have a mastery of the English language? Why is it unusual for a man from the inner city to be an intelligent person and an accomplished communicator? It is unfortunate, but nevertheless true, that I battle the false assumption that because I grew up poor and black in one of America's most dangerous cities that some think I should be a cold-hearted, drug-dealing thug. It saddens me that when I tell people I am from East St. Louis, they do not believe it's possible I could have been raised there. That said, if I had been raised elsewhere, maybe I would have similar questions. We need to change the assumptions we make about people based on race and gender and other factors that are irrelevant to the content of a person's character. Many times we fall short of the value a person may hold because of the premature conclusions we make about them before learning who they really are.

The truth is that no one in this world succeeds alone, and no one fails alone regardless of their race. The more difficult the circumstances one finds themselves in, the more they need both strong personal character and the help of family and friends to make it through.

East St. Louis is a place America can learn from in many ways. It is a textbook example of how to create urban blight in the midst of prosperity through corruption in government, deliberate neglect, and the de facto segregation of a racial minority into an environmentally degraded and economically challenged city.

But my hometown is much, much more.

It is a place where every minute of every hour, every hour of every day, someone with very little reaches out and helps someone else with even less.

It is a community where people simply refuse to give up on each other. With an almost blind faith, they continue to battle for a better future.

It is a city that simply refuses to crumble.

With the love and support of my community, my family, and friends I also refused to crumble.

I knew what I wanted out of life.

Even more, I believed that I was destined for success.

CHAPTER 4
MY REFUGE

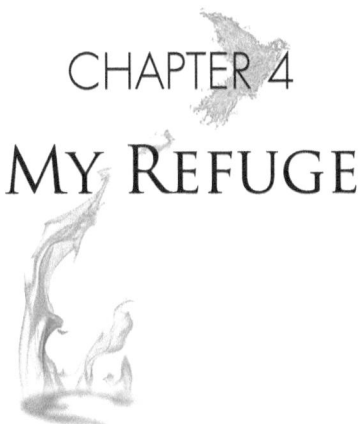

For as long as I can remember, school was a place of refuge for me. I not only felt safe in school, I was stimulated and challenged in a good way. At school, I not only learned about the world, and I am by nature a very curious person, but more importantly I was given the opportunity to interact with a great number of different people.

I was never the best and brightest student. My grades were consistently above average, but academic achievement never came easy for me. Unlike others, I had to work harder and sometimes longer.

Although no one knew it, my home life never left my mind and played a significant role in my school performance in both positive and negative ways. I worried about the possibilities of what would happen at home after school. I also thought about the sometimes tough events at home from the previous night. On the other hand, I knew at a tender age that school was the way out of my brutal environment. I had seen others in my extended family go off to college, get degrees, and go on to live productive lives. Education would open doors that would allow me to live like the people I saw on television. I reminded myself of this often. In order to survive, you have to keep reminding yourself that there is something greater and better for you in this life while you are going through your storm. This was my way of turning my negative environment into a positive motivation to succeed.

Literally from the time I started my elementary education at Warren Harding as a first-grader through my senior year at East St. Louis High School, I was happiest when I was at school.

I lived most of my time at my dad's house during those early years, and I walked from there to school every day. My first real best friend was Darnell Wilson who lived down the street from me and not far from the home of my father's wife, Beverly Price. Darnell was two years older than me. We played outside every day after school when the weather cooperated—kickball, football, or basketball. For a few years, we were inseparable.

What I remember most about Darnell was that he had a rough relationship with his stepfather. He would get booted out of his house from time to time, and I would wake up in the middle of the night and he would be sleeping on the side of my bed. Nobody knew he was there except for me. I left the window open for him, so he could come and go as he pleased.

This experience truly showed me that my father's good traits were rubbing off on me. I felt like a true friend. To me, the definition of a friend is someone who is there for you when you need them to be. He needed me, and I did whatever I could to help him.

I remember other friends from those days, Brandon Davis and his little sister Cierra Randolph, and also Tia Smith. We were all in the same boat, black children growing up in an economically depressed, crime-troubled community trying our best just to be youngsters and have a good time whenever we could.

I met Tia in second grade at Harding. Her house was another place of refuge for me growing up. When I was really young, I had a crush on her, but we were, and always have been, nothing but great friends. We spent countless hours hanging out and doing a whole lot of nothing.

Brandon was a basketball junkie. He loved playing on his portable goal and at the Salvation Army's gym, where they would let you play for a quarter. Brandon and I would catch the bus to the mall or the trains over to Union Station in St. Louis just to get away from home.

As the years went by, I lost track of Darnell and Brandon. Sadly, not long ago Brandon Davis was murdered outside of a local club, shot multiple times. I do not know what type of life he had been living because I had not been around him. We had just got back in touch with each other weeks before he was stolen from us, and we were scheduling time to finally meet. I never saw him again.

Brandon's death was very sobering to me. He was a father, son, brother, uncle, and an excellent friend. He was a loved and valued human being, but you will never hear about his murder on the national news. Too many people have become desensitized to the violence that has plagued my city for so long. They turn a blind eye to it because in some way they feel it is expected. This approach is misguided and misplaced and, at its heart, is an underlying prejudice that the lives of black Americans are just not as valuable as other lives. Like most East St. Louis residents, several people that I knew growing up are now dead, taken prematurely from this world in acts of senseless violence. Brandon is but one sad example.

However back then, in the mid-1990s, I really didn't know any better, as the expression goes: It all seemed normal to me.

Beverly Price loved me like I was her own. When I think about it now, it's amazing because she had every reason to resent me. I was the son of her husband's mistress. Not once in my entire life has Beverly Price shown me anything but love. I have always called her "Momma Beverly." She provided for me, and I always felt like I was a part of her household.

Our outings became almost ritualistic when I was younger. I would walk across the field to her house, or in the alternative, she would pick me up. Then our day of shopping would begin. I never knew that trips to places like Wal-Mart and Dress Barn could be so fun. The best place we went was the Dollar Store because this is where I would rack up all the toys. Each time I went in that store, I came out with a different superhero equipped with the proper gear. We would always top off the trip with a meal. Ponderosa Steakhouse was our favorite. Looking back now, it was not about the "stuff," it was more about the time that she spent with me. I was her baby, and she would move heaven and earth in order for me to have what I needed. Beverly Price was my safety net.

In my younger years, Momma Beverly would attend my school award banquets and programs. She was a rock of consistency that I could always turn to in a chaotic world.

Beverly Price became my surrogate mother. I began to confide in her in ways I wish I could have with my own mother. In my mind, I believed that God had sent me a supplemental mom to be there for me while my mom was away. I accepted it and counted my blessings, but initially I am not sure that my brother Smokey was fond of my close relationship with Beverly. I was the kid his father conceived out of wedlock with another woman, and his mom was giving me a great deal of attention. With time though, he grew to love and accept me as his brother, just as his mother accepted me as her very own child.

My mother Pansy was also a part of my life during this period, but her drug addiction was raging. I never knew if she would be home or not. Looking back now, I understand how hard life was for her, how she battled her demon, crack cocaine, and always lost. When you are 6 or 7 years old, you do not think in those terms, all you know is that your mom isn't around and you miss her and wish that she was well, happy, and sober.

Pansy would simply disappear for weeks at a time. She would say, "I'm going to the store" and days later, my dad would have to chase her down at a stranger's house or bail her out of jail.

There were times when my mother cleaned up and did her best for me. She and my Grandma Bertha would take Crystle and me to church. When I was 8 or so, I was baptized at the New Bethel Missionary Baptist Church. For a time, I remember singing in the choir and going to Bible study at New Bethel.

I fell in love with Sunday school and Bible study. I already had a passion for learning, so I just applied that to my spiritual life. I would read a scripture and want a deeper understanding of the text. My faith is based on the scriptures more than anything else.

I was a praying person even as a young boy. I went through so many tough challenges as a child and through these trials, I learned that I always had God to turn to and that He would comfort me. While I've never been caught up in religion per se, either as a youngster or now, I believe in God and in the saving grace of Jesus Christ. My faith in God is truly my foundation.

When all else failed, I knew prayer could break any bondage that the enemy tried to put me under. I knew at a young age that God was raising me up for a greater purpose because he never let me stray too far off course. When I was younger, I found myself in some situations that could have gone bad fast but were resolved. For instance, I was with one of my buddies at a friend's house, and minutes after I left, I heard shots fired. I am grateful for the grace I was given when younger, but I always wondered if God heard me crying out for help, especially when I got on my knees and begged him to bring my mother back home to me.

My father was drinking his fifth of gin a day, while I was learning my ABCs at Warren Harding. He was there for me always, but it was tough to be around him when he was drinking.

As the oldest child in the home, it seemed as if I took the brunt of my father's fury when he was drunk. He was consistently angry when he was drunk. I never feared that he would hurt me to the point of hospitalization, but his slaps and punches penetrated my heart more than my skin. I felt life was hard enough already without having to deal with fighting off his blows. If those "walls could talk" at my dad's house, you would hear me cry and beg God to stop my father from hitting me.

Because Beverly and other family members and friends all lived within a reasonable walking distance from my dad's house, I always had somewhere to go. While craziness was all around me, I went about the business of being a little kid the best I could.

Growing up, I was very close to Crystle, Baby Robert, and my youngest sister Piatra. I was also close to my three older brothers—half-brothers—Paul, Chris and Robert Price III, or Smokey as everyone in the family calls him.

When I got a little older, 8 or 9, life got even tougher.

That's when we lost Chris.

CHAPTER 5

BROTHERS FROM ANOTHER MOTHER

Paul Price was born in 1967, when Beverly was a teenager. Dad and Beverly became a couple in 1969 after she was pregnant with Chris. Chris was born in 1970 and came along just before my father was sent to fight in Vietnam. Robert Price III, or Smokey, was born in 1973 when Dad got back from overseas.

Smokey grew up avoiding trouble and excelling in school. He went to college in Tennessee and got a degree in computer programming. He met his wife Stephanie in undergrad. They are happily married, and they have a daughter, Kayla. By the time I was 6 years old or so, Smokey was gone. I loved it when he came back home for visits, which he did from time to time. Mostly because I wanted to be like him, I grew up believing that I would also someday become a computer programmer. I did whatever I could to learn the craft.

Just like Smokey, I wanted to get an education and make a good life for myself. He made me believe that it was possible, that I could do it if I just put my head down and kept moving forward with confidence. Although Smokey does not want to live in the East St. Louis vicinity, he is exploring different ways to help the city from his home in Tennessee. Unlike me, he has no plans to live in the vicinity like I am. He has a family of his own and a flourishing career. I miss him and I would love to see Smokey more often than I do.

When I was a teenager and he came home, I would drop everything and go see Smokey. I wanted to be around him and hear his stories about college. However, I did not know early on that Smokey disliked me. He did not have disdain for me as a person per se. More so, he disliked that I was the product of a union that solidified his mother and father's separation. I was the physical manifestation of Dad's and Beverly's broken marriage. Over time, he grew to love and accept me as his little brother. When he would come home I would never let him isolate himself away from me enough to let those negative feelings fester. I am a firm believer that love conquers all. Now, we could not be any closer.

Smokey grew up with an atypical childhood for a kid in the inner city. He was very involved in many social programs, such as summer camps and extracurricular activities. School was his passion. More importantly, Smokey was able to be a kid. He did not have to worry about where the next meal was going to come from or if the lights would be on at home when he got there. As simple as it sounds, this is the reality that many kids face in a place such as my hometown. I faced it. Those worries overflow into every area of life. Smokey enjoyed this security because my dad and Beverly worked, and neither had a drug addiction while he was a child. He had "normal parents," per se. He was able to thrive. In fact, by the age of 10, he had his own bank account and understood the value of saving money. I did not have one until I went off to college.

There were other fail-safe systems in place that kept Smokey out of trouble. He was able to get great advice from his grandparents when he was younger. Dad was around more often to help him grow into a man. More importantly, when the streets tried to sneak into Smokey's life, Paul and Chris were there to nip it in the bud.

I yearned to soak up every new vocabulary word he had to offer me. As far as I was concerned, Smokey was a millionaire that had found his piece of the American dream. He graduated the No. 1 male in his class in high school and was in college studying computer science hundreds of miles away from East St. Louis. At that time, he was the smartest and most successful person I knew.

Paul and Chris took a different path. When they were younger, my brothers were tough men who were not afraid of confrontation. They also did not shy away from criminal activity. Drug dealing and engaging in other nefarious activities was a way of life for them. To this day, when certain people discover that I'm Paul and Chris' younger brother, I'm given immediate respect, "street cred."

However, what many people don't know about both of them is that before their life of criminal activity, they were stellar students. In fact, my mother, Beverly, still has some of their early report cards that attest to how intelligent they were academically. This is not just true of Paul and Chris, but of many inner city kids surrounded by multi-generational poverty and crime. According to Beverly, when Chris was in high school, she would drop him off for school every day at the front door, and he would go out through the back door as soon as she pulled away. He felt that he had already mastered the material he was being taught, so he was bored. Shortly after Chris began avoiding school, he and Paul became involved in the street life.

I thank God that Paul has pulled himself out of the cycle of arrest, conviction, doing time, being released, and getting arrested again. So many men in my community fall into this trap. The lucky ones, such as Paul, eventually extricate themselves and live in peace.

The less fortunate ones, like Chris, end up in a grave.

Christopher Price's State of Illinois Defendant's Criminal History Report, his "rap sheet," is nine pages long. Beginning in 1990, it is mostly filled with traffic citations, possession of small amounts of marijuana, and other misdemeanors. There are more serious crimes in his record—battery, illegal possession of firearms, unlawful use of a weapon, etc.

When I look at Chris' criminal history, the thing that makes me the saddest is this—he was arrested on several charges on November 2, 1997, including a felony charge. On November 6, 1997, Chris was murdered.

If only he had not made bail...

The morning of November 6, 1997, five men sat around drinking alcohol and smoking weed. One of them came up with a bright idea, "We should rob somebody today." It is these types of simple ideas that lead to massive pain and sorrow for so many people in the inner city and surrounding areas. The five men were DeAlandus Best, James Bean, Brian Hill, Gary James and Willie Springer. After some collaboration, they decided their target would be Gerald Little. They believed he would be ideal because they thought he was rich. Gerald was a known local drug dealer, and at the mere age of 24, he drove a BMW and was believed to always carry large amounts of cash on him. Unfortunately for my family, he was also an associate of my brother Chris. This relationship proved fatal.

So the planning began. They agreed that they would lure Gerald over to the house. Two of them would stay in the house, and the other two would lie in wait behind the house. One of them from inside the house would go make sure Gerald had drugs or money with him, and he would signal the others to ambush him. The other co-conspirator in the house would communicate with the ones in the back via walkie-talkie. When they thought the plan was airtight, they started gathering supplies for the heist. The robbery scheme was quite elaborate and involved obtaining black attire, ski masks to conceal their identities, and walkie-talkies.

The best laid plans of mice and men often go awry.

Around 6 p.m., Hill and Bean went to the side of the house; and Best went to the backyard. They were all armed. The arsenal of weapons included a .357 Magnum, .380 handgun, two 9mm handguns, and an AK-47 assault rifle, but the plan was that no weapons were to be fired, and no one was supposed to be shot. Gary James expressly told James Bean to be sure not to fire the 9mm because it was registered. The best laid plans of mice and men often go awry.

The wild card they weren't counting on was my brother arriving with Gerald. Chris and Gerald were criminal associates. I have no doubt that Chris was there as muscle for protection. Robbing drug dealers is a very common crime in East St. Louis, and no doubt Gerald was attuned to the risks of his profession. This is a clear example of why you have to be careful with whom you choose to associate. The wrong friends can lead to funerals on the same day. Here is how it all went down, based on what I know and official records.

Chris pulled up in his truck with Gerald in the passenger seat. Gerald got out of the truck. When the three in the backyard saw this, they panicked. They had planned for Gerald to be alone, and they recognized my brother. Chris had a "do not mess with" reputation. It was well known he was very dangerous. Rather than wait for the signal and then ambush them, three of the co-defendants from the backyard rushed Chris and Gerald. Those men were James Bean, DeAlandus Best, and Brian Hill. The best laid plans of mice and men often go awry.

The ambush was on. With their guns drawn, they ran from behind the house and ordered Chris and Gerald to put their hands up. Gerald ran as soon as he saw them. They chased him and knocked him down. Chris tried to pull off in the truck, but DeAlandus Best held him at gunpoint and ordered him to stop. They ordered Chris and Gerald not to move, but Gerald began moving. Then the first shots of that night rang out. James Bean shot Gerald twice in the legs. Gerald fell on his back and tried to get away. It is believed that James Bean went into shock after he shot Gerald because he looked like he was out of it. Gerald used his arms to pull himself down the driveway, across the street, and into a field across the street. Two of the men dragged him back across the street into the driveway. He was alive; kicking and fighting for his life. They picked him up and tossed him in the back of Chris' truck like a rag doll.

Brian Hill and DeAlandus Best jumped into the back of the truck to hold Gerald at gunpoint, and James Bean got into the cab with Chris and ordered him to drive at gunpoint. I believe that Chris knew at this point that these guys were not going to just let Gerald and him go, and that James Bean was probably going to make him drive to some remote location. I know the most prominent thing that was probably racing through his mind: survival. It was either fight or flight.

Chris hit the accelerator trying to flee and broadsided another vehicle in an intersection, sending the men in the back of the truck tumbling onto the pavement. After the crash, Brian Hill hopped out and ran to the streetlight about two feet away. He shouted at James Bean, which must have awoken him. James Bean got up and started shooting. James Bean shot Chris several times with the .357 Magnum as my brother was trying to flee. James Bean ran over to Brian Hill, and then they remembered that DeAlandus Best was still in the back of Chris' pickup truck. Brian Hill instructed James Bean to go get him, but at that moment they heard gunfire. They knew it was DeAlandus Best shooting. This time, there were 10 or more shots. Apparently, Gerald Little had tried to roll under the truck attempting to avoid the gunfire, but he was unsuccessful. He and my brother were both pronounced dead at the scene.

The pathologist indicated that Chris had 13 wounds, six of which were recovered projectiles from his body. Four wounds were fatal. If Chris had lived, he would have been paralyzed from his wounds. He died from the wounds to the head, chest, and abdomen.

Soon after the crime, James Bean and DeAlandus Best were arrested and charged with two counts of murder. They are both doing life in prison and will very likely never breathe free air again. The other defendants pleaded to lesser charges in exchange for their testimony.

As a prosecutor, I have seen many cases like this, senseless acts of homicide committed because men were trying to steal a few thousand dollars from another criminal. It is a vicious cycle that is repeated too often.

But in 1997, I experienced this as a 9-year-old little boy. Chris' death broke my heart. I loved him as much as I loved Paul, Smokey, and Baby Robert. It was horrible, like a nightmare, only it was all too real.

The night of Chris's murder was surreal to me. The ammunition hitting the table and the gut-wrenching screams bellowing off the walls shook me out of my sleep. When I went into our kitchen, I saw gun cases scattered throughout the room like an abandoned army surplus store. My uncle told me that my brother had just been shot. Now it all made sense to me; my family was prepared for war and all I could do was pray.

I fell to my knees and began to ask God to save my brother, but it was too late because he had already passed. As bad as the situation was, my family and I were forced to move on because there was no escaping the brutal environment in which we lived.

My dad took my brother's death really hard, but I wish he had stopped drinking long enough to say, "Courtney, I love you." That never happened. Instead he showed his love by forcing my mother and me to shield ourselves from his alcohol-induced punches. It was then that I learned the only way for me to make a difference was to become a positive influence for my siblings and others around me.

A year earlier, I had lived through another bad dream. That's why Paul was not around to comfort me when Chris died.

Paul was in prison.

On September 26, 1996, my sister Crystle and I were sitting in the living room of our dad's house playing Super Mario Brothers on the Nintendo. We were waiting for the Project Success van to come and pick us up. Project Success is an East St. Louis community program for at-risk kids. In the afternoon, they would come by and take us to their facility, which was like an extended school. We did our homework and participated in group activities. Crystle and I both looked forward to going to Project Success every day.

But on this day, Paul walked into the house and shouted, "Dad, they comin'!" My father was home along with his friend Richard, who I called Uncle Richard. Paul was living in the little house on the back of my dad's property. No doubt he was manufacturing and selling drugs from this little house as well.

Suddenly there were 20-plus cop cars on Dad's property and dozens of armed men busting down doors and yelling and screaming. I remember one of the officers saying, "Nobody told us that there were going to be kids here." Mom was gone as I recall. The police arrested my father, Paul, and Uncle Richard, but Dad and Richard were released a few days later and not charged.

Paul was charged and convicted of Unlawful Delivery of a Controlled Substance and sentenced to eight years in state prison.

Crystle and I watched as the Project Success van pulled up to the crime scene that was my father's house that day and quickly sped away. Grandma Price was called, and she came and took us to her home.

Strange as it sounds, I was never scared during the whole drama. I actually thought it was funny. I remember sitting on the couch laughing at it all. In a very real sense, I wasn't a kid, I'd seen too much. I grew up way too fast. But of course, this wasn't funny. It was tragic. This was my defense mechanism kicking in. After a long period of time, it is easy for a person to become desensitized to the violence and misfortunes surrounding them. It is this reason why it is so easy for me to understand why the murder and drug rate is skyrocketing in the inner city. When you are surrounded by violence and drugs 24/7, it becomes a way of life for you whether you like it or not. It is up to you to break out.

In 1996, I lost one brother to prison, and in 1997, I lost the other to the grave. Smokey was long gone, living his life elsewhere. I was left to look over my younger siblings.

Before they were taken down, Paul and Chris Price together had been a force. Nobody messed with them, to do so would be suicide. My father taught them how to handle themselves in a fight, and by example, he sent them the message that being angry and violent was an acceptable way to behave.

I can close my eyes and see Chris doing the wildest things. One day, I was playing in front of my house and I heard screeching tires and sirens. Chris zoomed around the corner; half of his car was off the ground. He had the widest smile I've ever seen, the classic ear-to-ear grin. Right behind him were the Illinois State Police in hot pursuit. Chris loved every minute of it, like it was a game or something.

Yet for all their toughness and bravado, in the end Paul spent years in prison, and Chris only saw 27 short years of life.

You cannot be a gangster and not pay the price. Eventually the life will get you, one way or another.

My brothers learned that lesson the hard way.

I learned from them and many others that I wanted nothing to do with being a gangster. I wanted something different—what Smokey had.

I just wish someone would have been able to reach them when they were younger and tell them being wild is not the way to live. The easy money is really not easy. Like the Bible says, the path to destruction is wide and the gates of hell are always open.

It's too simplistic to say that being born and raised in East St. Louis "made" my brothers and, throughout the decades, thousands like them, pursue a criminal lifestyle. It's also naive to believe that if my brothers had been raised in a home with two stable parents and in a community where pro-social values were celebrated and law and order prevailed, that they would likely have made the same poor choices.

As a society, we can do more to help kids make better choices, before they become teens and young adults. I took full advantage of all of these types of programs and it helped me.

As individuals, we simply have to accept the fact that

actions have consequences. Choices lead to results.

In positive terms, we can become what we aspire to be. I'm living proof.

In Biblical terms, the wages of sin is death.

Chris Price taught me that lesson, God rest his soul.

Chapter 6
Alternate Path

When Chris died, my life could have easily changed for the worse. The rage and anger families feel when a relative is brutally murdered is insurmountable. This is enhanced in a culture where being protective of family members is held to be sacred. Many young people face these traumatic experiences at a very young age, and they go on to live a bitter life. Maybe you have experienced these feelings or emotions just as I did. For some, these types of traumatic events lead people down the road to gang banging, drug dealing, and being society drop-outs. Literally, it creates a cycle of criminal misfits. Revenge rules their hearts.

I want to give you a glimpse of whom and what I could have been. If my choices were different, the below hypothetical could be my present-day life.

****

Chris' death sent our family into a tailspin. All of his homeboys showed up to the funeral. They showed me all types of love. I wanted other people to show me that same kind of love. Chris had everything he wanted—money, women, cars—you name it, he had it. I wanted what he had. I figured that maybe if I'm just a little safer and use this brain of mine, I could make the same type of bank Chris did and then some. I decided then that the streets were my new home and slangin' dope was my new hobby.

At the funeral, I hooked up with one of Chris' homeboys, Rodger, who was deep in the game. Before, when he had seen me around the hood, he told me to stay out of trouble. Now I let him know I was finally putting the books down. I was ready to make some real money. He told me to think it over, and if I was sure to meet him at 1 p.m. the next day at the liquor store. We shook on it. The only problem was, I had to be at school the next day. Choices, choices, choices.

That night I thought about it. So many thoughts hit me all at the same time—my dad was struggling to pay bills, my mom was chasing her next high, my little sister deserved so much more than what was being provided, and on and on. I wondered what this life really was about. Why have I been sent here to suffer? Then it hit me, I wasn't. I was sent here to be a street legend. The hood was my kingdom, and the streets would play by my rules. My choice was made, and I had big hood dreams.

Even though I was still a kid, it only took a few months for me to get the operation down. Before I knew it, years had passed and my biz was running like clockwork. I had the little homies on the block selling rocks making me rich, just like I did when I started off with Rodger. I paid the police whatever I needed in order to stay in business. Feds ain't breathin' down my neck neither, not yet, and I got ways of knowing when they are comin' too. Even though I don't have the police hounding me, the little homies in the streets have been vying for the top spot and the word is that they are going to try to knock me off. I'm not trippin' though because I stay strapped with my 9mm. You know what they say: You live by the gun, you die by the gun. Messing with me, they were surely going to die.

Things were going well until Calvin, one of my foot soldiers, was stupid enough to carry both product and cash with him to a meet and got robbed. Ten Gs down the toilet! Then he cried like it's someone's fault other than his. I swear the man is 30 years old goin' on 13. But he's loyal, and he knows how to keep his mouth shut. After four arrests and a conviction without rattin' me out, I trust the dude. Still, he needs to grow a brain at times. All a cost of doin' biz I suppose.

Sometimes I wonder, ya know, what might have been. Once upon a time, I was a good student, loved school and all that. But after Chris got shot, man I just gave all that up. I mean, everything just didn't make sense anymore. Chris was the toughest guy I knew, and he wasn't careful one time and now he's gone. It's been almost 15 years since then, but I learned my lesson. You can't be too careful if ya want to get ahead in this world.

I've only been shot twice and neither was what you'd call real serious. Once I was just sittin' in my car with the boys watchin' a deal go down, and the bullets started to fly. I caught one in the shoulder. A quick trip to the backroom, some knife work and a few shots from the doctor, and I recovered quick enough. Second time, I took one in the leg when some dude wanted to shoot it out rather than pay what he owed. He got his coming though. Watch.

I've lost so many friends now, more than 10 guys cut down. Hey, when you live in the jungle, sometimes the tigers get a few of the tribe. Still, it sucks. I don't try and hurt anybody, I hate guns and violence but I live by a code—I won't hurt you if you stay outta my biz and keep your word. Don't always work out that way though.

I guess the real thing that's been botherin' me is my kids. I got three boys and a little girl now. I love 'em all, I really do. I don't get to see my oldest boy much because his mamma won't have anything to do with me. She gets all damn righteous about how her boy "isn't going to have a gangster for a father." Her new husband, him and I—let's just say his teeth are on temporary loan from my right fist. He does not know who he's talkin' to when he runs his mouth to me, but outta respect for Courtney, Jr., I swallow my pride and just take it. My two littlest ones are the best. Me and Shelly been together almost three years now. Other than her drug habit, she's a good mom. I guess I can't complain too much, it is what it is.

On that subject, no one can understand why I never

sample my own product. Oh, I'll drink with ya, not all that much, but I'll pound a few, no doubt. I just can't stand drugs, not even weed. I think people who use drugs are dumb, but I need them. They are my customers. Drugs are just messed up. I don't want my brain all foggy and doped up.

Ever since Mom got clean, she's been tryin' to get me to stop dealin' and go to church with her. She knows the scene, that's for sure. She keeps askin' me, "Courtney, how much money do you really need?" I got almost 300 Gs stashed in cash now. Sounds like a lot of dough, but really I should have three times that amount put away. How long would that last me anyway? I spend money as fast as I make it. Around town, I try and keep a low profile—I drive a 10-year-old beater, stay away from the clubs, and live low-key in this beat-up old house, but I got another life.

Couple a years ago, I bought a house in the country. I don't tell everyone about it, but enough people know—too many people for sure. It ain't in my name—I got it in a fake identity I had a pro set up for me. I like to go out there by myself or with the kids and Shelly. When I'm out there, it's like I live a different life in a different world. I dress different, and I have a nice new car in the driveway. I tell the neighbors that I'm a lawyer, and this is my country getaway place. I can fake bein' a lawyer quite well. I know the lingo and the names of motions and forms. When I was a kid, I dreamed of being a lawyer. No one asks too many questions. I know better than to crap where I eat, so when I'm out in the country I'm just a law-abiding citizen.

Yea, it's a dream. Make enough money, move away and, I don't know, open a legit business of some kind. I think I could do well as a businessman. Maybe somethin' to do with computers, I've always been a fairly decent computer guy.

But I got real problems right here that I need to take care of. All the daydreamin' in the world won't change that. I gotta business to run and it sure does not run itself. I just hate I have to watch over my shoulder every second in order to do it. I just pray I see another birthday. OMG . . . the police are at the door. My life is over.

Sometimes though I can't help but wonder what could have been . . .

****

What you just read about me could easily have been my life. In fact, I painted a rather rosy "what-if" picture for you.

Truth be told, if I had chosen to follow in Chris and Paul's path in the drug world and so many others' footsteps, I could easily be dead or in federal prison doing a three-decade stretch or more. I would not enjoy life as I do now in my comfortable home with my beautiful wife and daughter.

I never aspired to be anything criminal because I was able see the negative effects of that life around me. My mother and father battled drug addictions. My father's drug addiction partially ruined his first marriage. My mother's drug addiction killed her chance to be a great mother to her children. Chris was murdered, and Paul was behind bars. That life sure was not for me. It was not the danger that I feared, but more so the lack of a future. I always aspired to be a leader, and I had a heart to serve. Neither of those opportunities existed in street life.

Choices, it really comes down to choices. I thank the Good Lord every single day that I made the right ones, or at least enough of the right ones.

I pray every day for the many in East St. Louis and other cities like it who have chosen the wrong path.

CHAPTER 7

THE OTHER SIDE OF THE COIN

Despite their choice of an antisocial lifestyle, my brothers always supported me and encouraged me to do well in school and stay on the straight and narrow path. They helped me in any way they could. Both of them protected me from the dangers that were everywhere. No one messed with Paul and Chris' little brother. To some, it might seem strange that my brothers chose to sell drugs, but at the same time did not want their siblings to be a part of their criminal enterprise.

Fortunately, for me, that was the case. Even though I was surrounded with drugs and money, my brothers never encouraged me to be a part of that lifestyle. There is a strong possibility that my life could be very different if they had, as I've previously shown you. Unfortunately, this is the case for many inner city youth. Growing up in a place where drug dealing is a flourishing business, it is easy for kids to idolize the kingpins and want to be just like them. Usually, drug dealers have all the necessities a kid may be missing in life such as food, clothes, and shelter. But it is much more elaborate in many cases. This is even more intensified when those kingpins are your brothers.

As a bystander, I have seen many things in the drug world. My home at one point was a hub for this activity. Either drugs were being sold by my brothers or my mother was buying them from random drug dealers through the night. This was my life as a young child. The money is fast and plentiful. The street glamour is attractive. For most young boys, the women are bountiful as well, given his status on the streets as a kingpin. So, if you are living in the projects with parent(s) on welfare that may not even have a car . . . Why wouldn't you want to sell drugs? This is the scenario that many of America's inner city youth face daily.

I never was tempted. My brothers never insisted that I get involved in drug activity. After Paul was arrested and Chris was murdered, I knew it was not the life for me. I loved school like my brother, Smokey. But that raised an interesting question for me: What happened to Paul and Chris, and why did they choose the streets? As stated before, they were excellent students. What made them turn to the streets instead of corporate America? I think I might know the answer.

It was disclosed to me that as a young child Chris was never satisfied. He always wanted things his way or not at all. In fact, if he wanted something and he did not receive the exact item, he would decline it all together. In the alternative, he would just destroy it. He wanted to live life with no limits, and he did. Unlike me, Chris had all his necessities given to him. He had hood dreams. When I was younger, he told me that he made $5,000 in one night. Drug dealing was the key in supporting his lavish lifestyle. He had it all: cars, money, jewelry, an arsenal of weapons, and women. He also lost everything, and we lost him.

Paul on the other hand is a different story. He was the oldest brother and a protector. He had his first child when he was 18. He was expelled from high school for a gang altercation, but went to the Job Corps to get vocational training. The drug life was a lifestyle for a time, but at some point, it became a supplement for his everyday living. Unlike Chris, Paul always worked a steady job as a chef. He never lived a lavish lifestyle and never became overly dependent on the profits from drug money. To that point when Paul was selling, he would use the money to pay bills at his home or support a legal business venture, while Chris lived with Beverly and had minimal responsibility even though he was a young father as well.

While they both were involved in criminal activity, they were worlds apart in my eyes; although in the eyes of the law, they were exactly the same. To me, however, they were just my brothers. I was too young to fully grasp the implications of their actions. I knew drug dealing was wrong, but I didn't know the full spectrum of the people affected by it. It crimped my family and devastated others. Drugs have become a new form of slavery in the inner city. The dealers are enslaved to the profits, and the users to their next high.

So many young men end up in this trap. But I wonder, why? How does a kid choose the streets instead of the classroom? If you're an outsider, then you might think that this is a complicated choice, but in many cases it is not. My brother Paul told me the only reason he didn't go to college was because nobody ever explained to him what college was. If somebody would have told him, he would have enrolled. For him, it was that clear. Sometimes the choice is as simple as parents are not able to afford stylish clothes or shoes that a kid might want, or be able to give them cash to go do fun things. Poverty is partially the culprit in these circumstances. It is the lack of these items in most cases that entices kids to want material items more, and want them now. This is especially true when others around them have those things.

A lack of supervision is another factor to be considered in determining why a child chooses to sell drugs. In many cases children are left to raise themselves, and sometimes this is not on purpose. Parents must often work multiple jobs and they are not there to provide guidance to their children. I recall a time where I was living with my father, and my mother was incarcerated. It was just me and him. My other siblings were living at my grandmother's home. He worked the night shift in which he went to work at about 4 p.m., and I got out of school at 3:30 p.m. Thus, there was a period of time that I was making the decision about how my day and night would be spent. Unlike me, Paul, Chris, and Smokey had all their necessities provided to them. Beverly and my father both worked full-time and were away from home very often. In fact, my father worked two jobs. You would think this would be the formula for success. However, this absenteeism also played a role in why Paul and Chris started selling drugs. Technically, Paul as the oldest raised Chris and Smokey. Without much guidance, Paul turned to the streets and so did Chris. This choice forever altered their futures.

Growing up, I always looked up to my brother Paul. After he got out of prison, he lived with us for a while, and then rented a house nearby. Before too long, I had a room and a house key. By the time I reached high school, he had become my best friend. In some ways, he treated me like his equal. I spent a lot of time with him growing up. He was able to instill direction in me, while my father was out working for the family. I respected his opinion because I knew that my brother had my best interest at heart. I had always longed to have a consistent male figure in my life, and my brother, Paul, filled that void on a regular basis. The same person that society had condemned had taken me under his wing and kept me out of trouble.

And in turn, in a way, I helped him as well. I became his "new" little brother to care for. In no way could I replace Chris nor did I try, but in some way I filled a void for Paul and Beverly. An everyday piece of their lives had been stolen from them, and I was there to help ease their pain. It was amazing to see Paul transition from street life to the straight and narrow life. I was there when he was baptized and gave his life to God. His life reaffirms my point that if you choose a good, wholesome life you can have one. This can be obtained even if you come from a prior criminal lifestyle. Now he is working and providing for himself legally. I admire his work ethic, and I am grateful for all he has done for me.

CHAPTER 8
A New Beginning

After Chris died, I became even more immersed in school and after-school activities. I had no other positive option. By then, I already knew that "hangin' out on the streets" was not where I needed to be. It was either spend my time in school or spend my time at home. Unfortunately, Dad's house was just not a healthy, uplifting place most of the time.

Until my father quit drinking in 1997, when I was 11, I had to be careful around him. When my mom was around, it could literally be chaos. The best way for me to avoid violent outbursts from my dad and crazy scenes with my mother was simply not to be home unless it was time to eat or go to bed. Of course, I could always go to Grandma Ernestine's house, but I didn't live there, I lived with my dad.

I recall times where if I did not obey the way he wanted, he threw random items at me. I feared him, but I also wanted to make him proud of me. Every boy wants to please his father, and I was no different. I wish every father felt the same way about pleasing their sons. Through my dad's actions, I got the clear message that he didn't care about pleasing me. Sadly, before he quit drinking, I felt at times he cared more about where or who was going to buy his next fifth of gin than he did about his son's happiness.

Many fathers have this notion that if they provide for their family financially, their job is complete. This is false. There is an emotional element to a father's love that sons and daughters need to fully develop. Unfortunately, this was lacking in my life.

So I became involved in clubs, organizations, and sports. My teachers were my lifeline to sanity, an escape from the madness, and a window into a world I desperately wanted to join. Even before middle school, I had become attached to more than one teacher, especially female instructors. Looking back, I understand what I was really searching for was a substitute mother—someone to love me, guide me, and tell me that I was worthy.

In grade school, my substitute mom was Ms. Jane James. Ms. James took a special interest in me, and sent me to a college summer program. Belleville Area College, now called Southwestern Illinois College, offered a program where kids could come and visit the college for a few weeks in the summer. The idea was to expose youngsters such as myself to higher education, to the possibility of a life beyond the tough neighborhood where we lived.

We built and launched model rockets and even

constructed a voice-activated robot scooter at Belleville Area College. These were the types of things I wanted to do with my life—to be a creator, an achiever, someone who excelled. Ms. James helped me to clarify my vision for my life, and she encouraged me.

Ms. James was the first Caucasian person with whom I built a genuine relationship. As I previously mentioned, East St. Louis is 98% African American, and I had not journeyed far outside its boundary. Jane James saw something in me I did not know that I had—potential. My relationship with her was strange to me initially because it flew in the face of what the streets had taught me—white people are the enemy. Through her actions, she proved this was a myth. She expressed her sincere opinion to me that I was college bound, and that one day I would be very influential. I believed her. Her words helped shape my views on the value of my education.

In middle school, I latched on to Mr. Glen Norwood. Mr. Norwood was a science teacher. I marveled at his understanding of the natural world. He made the thirst for knowledge contagious. He sparked my desire to learn—to dig beneath the surface. More importantly, he introduced me to the Scholastic Bowl team.

Scholastic Bowl was the first intellectual activity to which I was exposed. Scholastic Bowl is a game of questions that spans many topics from sports to literature. Thus, you need a broad range of knowledge. Teams were made up of 4–5 players, and we had a buzzer system. A moderator would ask a question and just like any other game show, we would buzz in to answer the question to score points.

While I enjoyed Scholastic Bowl, there was not enough creativity associated with playing the game so I joined a Sim City competition. This was before the expansion of the video game Sim City. Our task was to build a city virtually, and then physically build the same city per scale in model form. The city itself was supposed to be one in the future with advanced technology. We presented our city at a competition at the St. Louis Science Center. I learned through this process that I loved creating things. I knew that I was competitive, but I did not know I was innovative as well. Therefore, I started to discover myself.

In the seventh grade I took up golf. Why? A golf course sat right next to my Grandmother Price's house. I started to hit some balls and soon found out I wasn't half bad at the sport. Today I love golf, but back then, my budding PGA career was cut short because I wanted to pursue another athletic option, football.

I'm a large human being and always have been. The coach of the Clark Middle School Cardinals convinced me that I had the ability to be a good player, so I joined the team. I was on the track and field squad as well. These teams provided much needed structure and consistent male role models in my life.

Family also provided plenty of positive role models and support. While my mom and dad had not yet gotten to the point in their lives where they could provide that for me, my grandparents, aunts, uncles, brothers, and cousins most certainly could and did.

Perhaps my greatest source of inspiration during those late elementary and middle school years was my brother Smokey. By then, he had finished his college education in Tennessee and was beginning his life as a computer programmer. Beverly was very proud of her son—and with good reason. He had freed himself from the trap of East St. Louis by his commitment to his studies. Smokey would come home and share all of his travel and life experiences with me. He had been to Japan and the Virgin Islands. I soaked up these stories like a dry sponge in a puddle. He challenged me mentally unlike anyone else around me. He made me expand my thoughts and views on the world as a whole based on the life he was living. I made the most of every opportunity to be with him because I planned on becoming every bit as successful as he was or more so.

During those years, I also saw a great deal of my Grandma Bertha, my mother's mom. She lived in Washington Park, which is not that far from my dad's house. While both she and Grandma Price were women of faith, it was Grandma Bertha who took me to church most often when I was younger. When my mother was there, during her brief periods of sobriety, I remember listening to her sing in church, and to this day, she has a beautiful voice.

My Grandma Bertha, like my Grandma Price, was the matriarch of her side of the family. Everyone on my mother's side would convene at her house for family gatherings.

Every Fourth of July weekend, the entire family would come into town and stay at her house. The majority of my family members on my mother's side lived out of town. Thus, my cousins did not grow up in the streets of East St. Louis. It was always great seeing my aunts and uncles and playing with my cousins. I was my grandmother's first grandson on that side of the family, which makes me the oldest male cousin. My cousin Steven Logan was right in line behind me. He is the son of my mother's sister, Jean Logan, who we called Aunt Jeanie. He has two sisters, Stephanie and Chelsie Logan. Out of all of my cousins, I saw them the most frequently. They only lived two hours away, and on occasions, my Aunt Jeanie would let us come and stay with her for a weekend. She is one of my favorites for sure. My grandmother Bertha believed in fairness, and she never showed favoritism among any of us. Also, she strongly believed that children should behave as such. We were not allowed to participate in adult conversations or activities like card games. She believed in decency and order.

More importantly, Grandma Bertha believed in family. The week before she died, she told me, "Courtney, I don't care what your mom has done. She is still your mother and the only mother you will ever have in this world. I do not like the things my daughter does, but she is still my daughter, and I love her. Love your mother even if you don't like her actions." I promised her that I would. I always have. I have replayed those words repeatedly throughout the years, and I have applied it in other ways in my life. There was a bigger lesson embedded in her statement; the lesson was that even people who do bad things or are addicted to drugs or alcohol at their core are still human beings. Everyone is worth saving regardless of how bad or far gone we think they might be. I think many times we forget this. I try hard not to.

My father's sister Brenda Acoff has three sons, Dwayne, Marcus, and Melvin. Dwayne pursued a military career and became a master sergeant in the Air Force. Marcus, like his cousin Smokey, also became a computer programmer. Melvin, their youngest, was older than me, and always there to help me whenever I asked. In fact, on par, he was my cousin that was around the most. He was older than me but not by as many years as Dwayne and Marcus.

From a distance, I thought that my cousin Dwayne was living a great life. Every time he came home, he would be driving a different luxury car. The important thing to me about it was, unlike Chris, he was not selling drugs to buy a new Mercedes. His brother Marcus was also doing quite well. He owned many rental properties. They both showed me that it was possible to reach a high level of success if I worked hard and stayed focused on my dreams.

Dwayne and Marcus made it in their own separate ways. Dwayne went into the United States Air Force and became an air traffic controller. Marcus went to college to become a computer programmer at Tennessee State University. He was enrolled there at the same time as Smokey. Both of them escaped with the help of many others.

Their mother, Auntie Brenda, and my Uncle Melvin (who died in 1990) were stable people who worked hard to raise their children properly, loved them, and provided a healthy home environment. She has always been an inspiration to me. She was very successful in life and did not obtain her bachelor's and master's degrees until recently. She has been a true example of how prosperous life can be if you have great integrity and excellent character. In every family there are people I consider "rocks." These are the go-to people in the family. She has been a rock for me all my life. We push each other, and although she would never admit it, we make each other better. She later remarried, and my Uncle Jack has been around most of my lifetime. I was always welcome in Brenda's house, and I would stop by often.

There was also my Auntie Barbra (deceased), my dad's oldest sister. As a younger child, I had many questions, and my Auntie Barbra did not hesitate to answer them. I would go to her for life and relationship advice. She would always give me the honest truth. She lived around the corner from my Grandmother Price's house. I spent a lot of time at her house with her son Kyle, who was a few years younger than me, when I lived at my grandmother's house in Golden Garden.

So between school, clubs, sports, and positive extended family members, I had a network I could plug into on a daily basis that supported my choice to be a success. In this regard, I was better off than most kids. I was lucky. The things that I lacked in my life were filled by outer positive resources and influences. The need for role models and mentorship programs is great. Many kids do not have anything positive to model their lives after. There are many that do not have these outlets, and this is part of the underlying issues kids face growing up in cities such as East St. Louis.

This literally saved my life because I was surrounded by serious problems.

No child should have to go to the county jail and visit his mother on a regular basis. Yet that is exactly what I did during these years. My father had, and has, an endless reservoir of love for my mother. He would bail her out of jail on this or that drug charge or, just as often, on a theft charge. My mother stole from area stores to support her drug habit. She even stole from us to support her drug addiction. I recalled working long days cutting grass or raking leaves in the neighborhood just to make some money to buy things and that money would vanish through the night. Items from our house would end up in local pawnshops because she needed money to get high. It was a very common event for my mom to disappear for days at a time, and for my father to have to search through the area crack houses to find and retrieve her.

I was 11 when my father quit drinking in 1997. Life definitely improved at home, but there was still a great deal of tension and nothing in the way of positive stimulation. My brother Paul remained in prison. Dad worked two jobs to support our household.

By middle school, many of the kids I knew in the

neighborhood were already getting arrested for drug possession and distribution, and property crimes. If I wanted to pursue that life, the "life" that killed Chris, it was literally just outside my door.

I believe that God always provides us with a door to walk through, a path to a righteous life. He certainly did that for me. The key is making the choice to walk through that door and having the necessary support around you to pick you up when you stumble. The choice element is the prime key to success. Everyone has or will have the opportunity to make pivotal decisions that will affect their future. Unfortunately, in tough environments, the negative choices are readily available and making the right choice is hard. We tell kids all the time to be wise in their decision making, but we do not take into account the outside factors that play a role in that process. Children who do not live in the inner city do not on average worry about violence, drugs, and lack of basic necessities. We treat it as though all kids are playing on the same playing field with the same equipment and coaches. This could not be any further from the truth.

However, by the time I was old enough to go to East St. Louis High School, I was more than ready to work hard and reach for the good life I knew God intended me to live. I chose to seek the most life had to offer, and I was not going to stop until I had it. Education would be my key to unlock all the doors to my dreams.

CHAPTER 9
THE KEY

The organization GreatSchools, Inc., a nonprofit educational school rating service based in San Francisco, gives East St. Louis High School its lowest possible rating, 1 out of 10. If you go to their website (http://www.greatschools.org/) and read the posted reviews and comments left by former students, parents, and teachers, you will find comments such as, "East Side is an out of control school. Neither the principal nor the teachers have any control over the school," and "This school is a haven of horrors! If you enjoy sending your child into a war zone where he or she will literally fight for his or her life then send them to East Side."

That's my school, and not much has changed since I graduated in 2004. It was, and remains, rough. I was shuffled through metal detectors every morning before given access to the school building. There were security guards scattered throughout the building for safety. It was and is a reflection of the community it serves. But there are other comments on the GreatSchools website about East St. Louis High School, including this one that entirely sums up my view of my alma mater, "I am a 1969 graduate of East Side, and three of my children are past graduates (1999, 2001, 2004). They are all productive, happy young men and women. They were taught by dedicated teachers and encouraged by caring members of the support staff. If a child has a sincere thirst for knowledge, shows a respectful manner toward their peers and respects authority, neither poor school administrators nor safety issues will interfere with their educational goals. This thirst for knowledge can be obtained by giving a child a safe place to learn that is free from distraction, basic needs met, and understanding the value of education. All teachers aren't teachers, all administrators aren't qualified, but if the parent and child are in one accord about the goals expected of them, their mission is less bothersome and their focus is clearer."

Like the Good Book says, "Seek and ye shall find." If you want to find gangs, drugs, crime, violence, everything that leads to unhappiness and personal destruction, then you can find it—in abundance—at East St. Louis High School. The sad truth is, you have to work hard to avoid these things, but it can be done. I recall a number of times when I witnessed students shooting craps or playing cards for money in the back of the classroom or in the bathroom. Then there were the more egregious things such as smoking weed in the bathroom while school was in session.

I'm living proof that it can be done, as are hundreds of other kids who not only survived their four years at East St. Louis High School but have gone on to prosper as adults. This includes average, non-scholastic kids as well. There are many doors to escaping an impoverished community such as sports, college, military, and acquiring trades. We have found many ways to survive and prosper. We did this by using our negative environment as positive motivation. There were teachers who helped us do that.

I found teachers at my high school who were not only competent, they were also caring. First on that list has to be Joyce Youngblood. She was a drama and civics teacher. Every student was scared of her. She had the reputation of being a "mean" teacher—supposedly impossible to please and looking to make life difficult for students. The truth was exactly the opposite. Ms. Youngblood believed, and rightly so in my view, that most of the kids coming to East St. Louis High School needed to be pushed academically and challenged with loving discipline. She took hold of me and would not let go. Ms. Youngblood even brought me food when she thought I wasn't eating enough. Her typical in-class policy was to allow students to eat in class because as she explained she did not know if a child had eaten the previous night. It was her understanding and creative teaching that made her one of the most effective teachers I had in my educational journey. She was my "mother" in high school, God bless her beautiful soul. I have gone back to speak to her students at East Side, to inspire them to achieve and be the best that they can be.

There was also Peggy LeCompte who taught honors English classes. She is known for her high standard of excellence. She would only accept a student's best work; excuses were not allowed. Every day in her class was like a job interview because we were expected to perform at the highest caliber. She forced the best out of us, even when we did not know it was happening. When I look back now, I understand that teachers such as Ms. Youngblood and Ms. LeCompte propelled me forward. These teachers would not allow me to be mediocre because they knew what type of world I faced before and after school. They knew the barriers that I would have to overcome to become a success in life. Schools with kids that face these types of issues thirst for such teachers, because they are able to reach kids right where they are. This enhances the learning process. I found the most effective teaching is tailored to the students that the teacher is responsible for, and I am lucky that some teachers that taught me employed strategies to reach me.

My football coach, Darren Sunkett, also knew all about overcoming obstacles. Our football team, the East St. Louis Flyers, has a storied history in Illinois high school football, having won the state championship over half a dozen times and the national championship twice. East St. Louis rallies around its team. Sports have always been something the citizens held on to even in the dark times. Every Friday night during football season when we have a home game, the stadium is packed. When I was a player on the team from sophomore to senior year, we began as a rebuilding program and ended up being ranked No. 1 in the state in my senior year and losing in the state semifinal game. The team we lost to my senior year went on to win the state championship.

Coach Sunkett taught me about discipline. He instilled confidence in me and allowed me to learn about consequences in a healthy way. Coach and I are still close. During football season, I spent more time with him than I did with my own father, which is typical of inner city athletes. He would pick me up and drop me off for practices. He would make sure I was not hanging with the wrong crowd. Coach provided the positive male influence that was lacking in my household. He kept close tabs on my grades and general well-being. I visited my first college and took my first road trip with him. Our team motto was "Expect Victory." I still walk in this expectation on a daily basis.

Children such as me who grow up in difficult environments can greatly benefit from participating in athletic programs. It gives kids opportunities mom and dad simply can't provide and access to places and experiences we wouldn't have otherwise. Unlike many other communities, positive role models such as doctors or lawyers are not usually found in East St. Louis families. Why do inner city kids idolize sports heroes? That's what they see all around them as examples of success. That's what they see when they turn on the television or open a magazine. What is unfortunate is that these kids don't realize that it is extremely difficult to become a professional athlete, only 1 in 100,000 athletes make it, but it is quite possible to become a doctor, lawyer, or business person. We need to do a better of job of giving our disadvantaged children more diverse role models and convince them at a very early age that the path to success goes through the classroom too, not just through the goalposts.

At this "rough" school, I not only played football, I was in the chess club, the drama club and on the bowling team. I threw the shot put and discus on the track team, and I was in the Beta Club Honor Society. I studied computer science and was able to take advanced courses, created just for me, on networking and routers while in high school. My extracurricular activities demonstrated that I was not a "one hat" type of person. I interacted with all types of people. I considered myself to be a "cool geek." I would hang with the football team one night and with the bowlers the next day. This was a very interesting dynamic. I was considered the glue that tied unusual people together. I found that we personally create walls of division based on our societal view of who we should be. For example, the athletes should hang out with the athletes, and the non-athletes should hang with the non-athletes, and there should not be any intermingling. I was able to bring them all together, and we always had a great time. In high school, I had a strong sense of who I was as a person, so I really never worried about what the football players would say if they knew I was hanging out with chess and drama club members. They respected me for my individuality.

I am not trying to casually dismiss the challenges that I and other kids faced trying to get an education at East St. Louis High School. Possession of weapons was common in school as were incidents of serious violence. Gang and neighborhood fights often disrupted the school environment. Any type of illegal drug was obtainable on demand.

In no way could this environment be considered a healthy one for children. Yet, despite all of these problems; despite the fact that many of the teachers had given up on themselves and their profession long ago; despite the fact that trying to stem the tide of criminal activity in the school was a never-ending exercise in futility, if a student wanted to avoid trouble and embrace learning, it was possible. If a person wanted to, it was possible to steer clear of trouble by ignoring those people engaging in that activity. No one forced their lifestyles on others. Most students surrounded themselves by other like-minded people.

That's the message the kids of East St. Louis and other cities like it need to hear and take to heart. Take control of your own life. Make good choices. No one is responsible for the choices you make other than yourself. Enough of these good decisions will ultimately lead to the right result. However, the other side of this coin, after a child has continually made those right choices we need to ensure they have opportunity and access. If not, those children will become hopeless. On top of everything else I was doing, I needed a job in high school. My parents were in no position to support me financially, and I wanted the same things every teenage boy wanted—a car, pocket money, and a taste of financial freedom.

Once more, family stepped up and helped me. Beverly Price's brother, Dan, was the manager of the galley on board the Gateway Arch Riverboat that gave tourists short cruises on the Mississippi. The riverboat docked right below the St. Louis Arch. Once I turned 16, during the summer and on some nights and weekends during the school year (while the season was still running), I worked on the boat as a deck hand. Employment opportunities are also important for breaking the cycle of poverty. Having a job instills a sense of responsibility and breaks the chain of dependency.

My first job was cleaning toilets on the boat. I gladly cleaned the restrooms, took out the trash and performed all of the grunt labor jobs I was assigned. I loved that job, I truly did. Not because I was a big fan of cleaning urinals but because I met so many interesting people. I would greet everyone with a smile and friendly hello. It was the first time I was exposed, on an ongoing basis, to a racially diverse group of human beings. It was a great opportunity for me to develop and hone my communication abilities, and I took full advantage. More importantly, the stories I heard from people who came from all over the world were fascinating and greatly expanded my personal horizons.

I recall a time when I met a nice couple from Brazil. I marveled at how they described their homeland. The scenery and images they placed in my mind made me want to visit their country.

I cherished the opportunity I had to work there. I was blessed with many intangible benefits from working on the boats. Perhaps more than anything else, working there widened my view of the world and introduced me to ideas and people I would never have encountered otherwise.

Originally, I used public transportation to get to school, but when I was hired I began to take it to work. Part of the way I had to walk, then grab a bus and then hop on a train. Many times I was plain old worn-out during those long summer days and nights. But it was worth it.

Toward the end of the football season in my senior year, I got my first car, a '99 T-Bird. I purchased it from my friend's mother for $1,000 from money I had saved up. To me, it was a Mercedes-Benz. It meant the world to me. Now my walking days were over.

Another great thing happened to me during my senior year. My brother, Paul, who by now was home from prison, gave me a key to his house, and I had a room there. No longer would I absolutely have to be a part of the drama at my dad's house. In fact, during my senior year of high school, I packed up my entire room at my dad's house and moved the furniture to the basement. I made the decision that I would never live in that room again. When I did sleep at Dad's, I slept on the living room couch. Although my dad had quit drinking, my mother was still completely addicted to crack cocaine. While I dearly loved them both, I was tired of having to live in constant turmoil.

I was ready now to move on. I got a football scholarship

to McKendree College, now McKendree University, in Lebanon, Illinois. It was located only 20 miles away from home and family, was close enough to my house and family, but far enough away from them to feel that I had broken free. My days of being a captive to my environment were over. My hard work and positive choices were about to pay big dividends.

Chapter 10
The College Experience

My first night of college was unreal. There were no gunshots or arguing. I had found my serenity. I was assigned to a suite that housed six football players. Sherman Ellington and Darron King were two of those players. We played alongside each other at East Saint Louis Senior High School. We sat there thinking, "What do we do now?" There we were: no one to tell us what to do, no one to wake us up in the morning for class. We were in the "real world," or so we thought at the time. For me, it was a major milestone. My other roommates explained to me that their parents were college graduates, their parents had saved money for their college education, and they always knew that they would be going to college. My story was the opposite. I was just happy to be alive and grateful that a college accepted me.

McKendree was a predominately white college and was the first college established in Illinois. The transition from an all-black community to a mostly white school and town was interesting. There were no stray dogs and cats, we did not have to lock our doors, and people felt overall safe. That was good, but the culture shock I felt was immense. I felt the pressure to assimilate into the new culture that surrounded me. After some time, my use of the English language was enhanced, my dialect began to change, and my exposure to the world had broadened. When I would go back to my neighbored, I got the typical, "Why do you talk white?" or "Why you acting like you white?" However, I did not let these things stop me from bettering myself. There was always an internal battle that raged inside me. It is basically the concept of "double consciousness," which is when a person's identity is split among multiple cultures. This idea was explored by W.E.B. Du Bois in his 1903 book The Souls of Black Folk. That is exactly what I was fighting. The internal battle centered on trying to stay true to myself, while accepting the fact that I was not perfect and could use refining in certain areas.

I struggled academically during my first semester. I knew that I was behind most of the other students based on what happened during orientation. On my first day, the instructor asked the students in the classroom to raise their hand if they had already earned advanced college credit in high school. Everyone in the room raised their hand except for me. I had no idea what advanced college credit even was. There were people coming into college literally skipping entire academic years.

Very quickly I learned that the disparity in the public

education system is real. While I believe that I got all I could from my years at East St. Louis High School, my lack of a good educational foundation was obvious. That first semester, I failed both math and English, not because I wasn't intelligent or working hard enough, but because I was ill-equipped to handle college-level writing and math. I bounced back quickly after being placed on academic probation and given a study skills class. I was now on my way. I refused to be sent back home—failure was not an option for me.

Initially, I went to college on a football scholarship. After playing for a semester, I quickly learned that football was no longer for me. Truthfully, I was not big or fast enough to become a professional athlete. I was able to keep my football scholarship for the duration of my tenure at McKendree, but I laid my helmet to rest. I paid a visit to the dean and explained to him that I did not want to play football anymore; I wanted to be more involved with other programs such as debate, Model United Nations and the student ambassadors. He agreed with my plan. It was tough walking away from football, but my life had come to a crossroads. It was time to use my brain more than my body.

My decision to stop playing football was pivotal. The other programs I became involved in proved to be the catapult to my intellectual success. My freshman year, I took an argumentative communication class. I enjoyed it more than I thought I would. I was encouraged by my teacher to speak with Joe Blasdel, then and now the coach of McKendree's

Speech and Debate Team, about joining the team. Joe allowed me to join with no prior experience. McKendree's Speech and Debate Team has won more national championships than any other organization on campus. I was thrilled by the chance to compete! It took me many long nights to get up to speed.

On every debate outing, I learned more about the world than I did during my entire four years of high school. I was honored that both my debate coaches, Joe Blasdel and Micheal Artime, welcomed me on the team and took me under their wing, despite my inexperience. I would go on to win three national Pi Kappa Delta team debate championships, including one my senior year with my partner Steve Loftus. We traveled the country weekly. We went to places such as Washington, Tennessee, Kentucky, and Kansas. I truly believe that without Joe and Michael, I would not be the person I am today.

Debate began my true transition from a hood mentality to a professional one. When I started debating, I didn't own a suit, and debaters were required to dress in business attire. I recall when I finally received my first suit. My grandmother Bertha purchased it for me. It was grey. Although unknown to most, this was a very special moment for me. My transition into the professional work field had begun, and I was another step further away from hood life. I cherished what that suit represented to me in my life. It was a minor but major milestone that I was happy to build on.

The type of debate our team did was named

parliamentary debate and was fashioned after the English Parliament. It was limited preparation. We would be given a topic and allowed only 15 minutes to formulate our arguments. Generally, there was no advance knowledge of the topic or topic areas. Thus, we were required to know what was going on in the world in order to be prepared to discuss anything they would throw at us. This was my jumpstart into the depths of the knowledge pool.

Model United Nations was another influential program. Many debaters competed in this program, so I wanted to be a part of it as well. Wow! That is all I can say. The largest competition was held annually in Chicago. I had never been a part of something so big before. Thousands of people came from all around the world representing their assigned countries. It was our task to take on the persona of our country. We had to know our country's position on global and domestic affairs and represent our country's interests in the Model UN General Assembly. Awards were given out based on the delegate's knowledge and portrayal of his or her country's political positions. I competed with this team for two years. During my senior year, I had the privilege of being assigned to the most influential section, the Security Council. This was based on my seniority on the team and my debate background. Needless to say, I learned many valuable skills by participating in the Model UN program—skills that directly translated to my future career as an attorney.

No student will ever tell you that college is just for

academics. I had fun in college. Nothing was more enjoyable than my experiences with my fraternity, Kappa Alpha Psi. My frat greatly expanded my network of friends. Since I went to a small liberal arts college with a limited African-American population, Kappa Alpha Psi gave me the opportunity to socialize with other young men that looked like me. Often my frat brothers and I would travel to colleges within a two-hour radius of McKendree and go to their parties.

The level of inclusion and bonding I felt in the fraternity was unlike anything I had experienced. I recall a time where one of my frat brothers was on the verge of dropping out of school because he could not pay his tuition completely. We took up a collection and gave him all of our book money so he could pay his tuition. This was the type of brotherhood that my African American fraternity was founded upon. More importantly, my love for my fraternity stems from our youth outreach and training program called Guide Right. The Guide Right program offers tutoring, mentoring, college/university visits, and social events for male high school students. It is so important that young children have role models and mentors. Steven Andrews, Leonard Johnson, Tyrus Armour, and Tyron Armour all members of my high school graduating class went on and became members of the fraternity as well. I have and will continue to dedicate my life to the betterment of the next generation.

Growing up, I wanted to be a computer programmer

like my brother Smokey and my successful cousin Marcus. All of my training before college was in that area. However, I changed my mind quickly after taking my first few computer programming classes. As it turns out, while I love hardware and using computers, I hated programming. Luckily for me, I was at a liberal arts college that allowed me to experience different types of classes. I changed my major seven times before settling on a double major in Communication and Philosophy.

My years at McKendree were a lot like the conversations I had with folks when I worked on the riverboats in high school. They were very intriguing and thought-provoking because they were people from different backgrounds and parts of the world. During my college years, I had roommates from Bulgaria, Jamaica, and the Bahamas. Even more astonishing, I met a number of Caucasian students who had never met or seen a black individual in person. These experiences allowed me to confront misplaced stereotypes and to educate people on my culture and community. In the same token, it allowed me to confront some ugly lies that I picked up over my years growing up in a 98% black community. I learned that all white people did not want negative things to happen to young black people. I learned that racial issues were bigger than just black and white racial harmony, but there were other minorities that were facing real problems as well. Interestingly enough, I slowly gathered that the white and black division line that I thought existed really was more so a rich and poor divide. It was not about color, it was about the all mighty dollar. Money determined your influence and access.

A common saying in the area is, "Don't go to East St. Louis." Many of my fellow students asked me, "Is it really that bad?" Early on in my college education, I became the official "Voice of Black America and East St. Louis." I recall countless times when professors made sly comments such as, "Nothing good can come from East St. Louis," without knowing that it was my city of origin. I always took these opportunities to challenge those harmful suggestions and assumptions. I have friends from my hometown who have attested to the same thing happening at their schools.

I met my future wife, Rachel, while I was in college. I met someone else too.

My little sister, Jamie.

CHAPTER 11

THE LITTLE GIRL AROUND THE CORNER

My heart was beating louder than the gunshots that so often echoed outside my window growing up. I stood in the hallway in a state of paralysis. Inching my way to the door, I began to tremble. I could not seem to summon up the strength to proceed. When I grabbed the door handle, I remembered what my forensics coach said to me before my debate duels, "Just breathe."

So I took a deep breath, moved through the door and came face to face with a classroom full of freshmen at East St. Louis High School. As they sat there with bare minds like mannequins waiting to be dressed, I allowed my feelings and thoughts to flow through my heart and form words. The sound of "Good morning" from my baritone voice broke the silent barrier over the classroom. It was my first time going back to my high school, and I was speaking to ninth-graders. I began speaking to ninth-grade classes during my freshman year at McKendree.

Going back gave me an opportunity to share my personal insights on the world where those students lived. I wanted them to consider a broader viewpoint on society. They needed help—some of them desperately needed help or else could easily pattern their lives after failures, not successes. I had no illusions—my going there and speaking to them was a small thing, but sometimes it's the little pushes in the right direction that turn the tide.

I wish there had been a person who cared enough to come and tell us about the consequences of making the wrong choices when I was sitting in those same seats. However, this was not the case. Many of my classmates over the years were either lost to the street or to the grave. Only 310 students graduated in my high school class that started with 615 students in my freshman year. I consider that to be a tragedy, but it's a tragedy that need not be repeated.

Before I began to speak, I looked into their eyes, and I felt a sense of brokenness. They were indeed reflections of me. Their daily existence in East St. Louis was saturated with poverty, crime, and unfortunate circumstances. I had a special understanding of what it was like to grow up poor and black in one of America's fallen cities. Life was dangerous, uncertain, and in a constant state of turmoil. I remember looking into my little sister Crystle's teary eyes and saying, "I will make things better, I promise." When I spoke those words, I was boiling water for her so she could take a hot bath. I felt that same urge to help these students when I looked into their eyes.

There was a beautiful young lady named Jamie Crocket in one of Ms. Youngblood's ninth-grade civics honors classes. She was a very intelligent and meek youngster. Ms. Youngblood made me aware that she was also gifted. When I would visit, I usually recited a poem or two that I had composed. Jamie told me that she wrote poetry as well. From the moment I met her in that classroom, I knew that Jamie was going to be a shining light in this world.

The next time I saw Jamie outside of my visits to the high school was in a college readiness program at McKendree. The program was called Associated Colleges of Illinois (ACI). This program is designed to prepare inner city high school students for college. I had participated in this program when I was a senior in high school. As a college student, I was given the role of student instructor.

Jamie was in one of my classes. When I looked closely at her, I couldn't help but notice that she resembled my mother. Then it finally clicked in my mind. This was not just a bright girl—she was my little sister.

Let's rewind to 1991. I remember waking up one day and discovering that my mother was missing. I thought she was up to her normal antics and that she would be home in a few days or weeks. This episode was different; she was gone for almost a year. The next time I saw my mom she explained to me that I had a little sister. During her absence, she became pregnant by a man she met in a treatment facility. I do not recall ever seeing her during her pregnancy; I didn't even know that she was pregnant. My sister was born

February 6, 1992. My mom named her Jamie.

The State of Illinois told my mom that she was not fit to have custody of Jamie. Mom could simply not bear to have another child taken from her, so she took Jamie from the hospital in the hope that somehow, some way, she could find a way to be with her daughter. She and the baby moved between friends' houses eluding the authorities for a while, but the FBI was on her trail so her hiding did not last long. Jamie was retrieved and placed in foster care.

I recall our visits with Jamie at a state-run facility. We would play with her all day until our visit time was over. It was *deja vu*. Now I was walking out on my little sister just like my dad did to me when I was a small child at the Catholic home. "What can I do, I'm just a kid?" I thought. Her caseworker would pack up all her belongings, and we left in separate cars. This went on for months.

Our visits ended when Jamie's foster mother applied to adopt her permanently. Mom could not meet all the necessary criteria to get her back. My father wanted to get custody of Jamie, but he couldn't because he was not her biological father nor had he signed the birth certificate. Her biological father was nowhere to be found and was also very likely unfit to be a parent. So, sadly for us, the state allowed her foster mother to adopt her.

The irony of the situation is that Jamie lived just around the corner from me. Only 783 steps, about seven or eight houses, two stop signs, and one school stood between me and my little sister. Growing up, I was not allowed to play with her or have any relationship with Jamie. I walked past her house for years wanting to stop and see her, but I knew that my efforts would be fruitless.

Her adopted mother seemed like she did not want us to be in her life, and through her actions, she enforced her will. Crystle and my little sister Piatra would take presents for Jamie to her home on her birthday and Christmas, but they were not allowed to personally give them to her. Once in a while, they would go to her home and try to play with her, but they were for the most part rejected. On a number of occasions, we attended her church services to try to see her. A part of me truly believes that her foster mother feared losing Jamie to the truth; the truth being that Jamie had siblings and a family that loved her dearly.

I did not make any attempts to see Jamie mostly because I could not handle the rejection. I could not understand how she could treat us in such a way. We were kids wanting to build a relationship with our sister, but it felt as if her adoptive mother treated us like we were predators. I had never knocked on her door for any reason; I knew one day Jamie would be old enough to make up her own mind whether she wanted us in her life.

Every year around Christmastime, we went to Our Lady of the Snow where they had thousands of Christmas lights decorating the trees. At the end of the display, they had a designated section where you could light candles and say a prayer. Mine was the same prayer every year, "God please send my little sister back to me." In His way and in

His time, the Lord answered my prayers.

I stood there in that class thinking that God has a strange sense of humor. I had spent hours speaking to Jamie's class not knowing who she was, but now I did. The window of opportunity had opened, and I was determined to go through it. The opportunity for me to build a relationship with my sister was now a real possibility.

I took Jamie aside and explained to her that I was her big brother. My revelation was a mystery to her. All her life Jamie was told that she was an only child. Soon enough, the pieces of the puzzle fell into place. Her adoptive mother could not have us around telling her that we were her siblings if she wanted Jamie to believe that she was an only child.

The news was a shock to her. I understood completely the mental anguish it caused. So, I gave Jamie my phone number and told her that whenever she wanted to talk about it just to let me know. That was the last class at McKendree that I recall Jamie attending.

Jamie has fulfilled all of the potential I saw in her when I first met her in that freshman civics class. She graduated valedictorian of East St. Louis High and went on to a college that has the best journalism program in the world. I could not be more proud of her. I believe that all things happen for a reason, and in a way she was sheltered from many of the hardships I had to endure growing up.

I enjoy every conversation that Jamie and I have. Our relationship is developing slowly but quite naturally. I am just happy that she is interested in talking to me and learning a bit more about our family. She has confided in me and expressed her feelings. Jamie felt abandoned and unloved by my mom—the same feelings I had when I was in foster care.

Recently, I was able to put Jamie and Mom on the phone with each other. Jamie was not prepared to say much, but she listened as our mom talked to her. Mom explained how she was very sick when Jamie was born, a victim of her addiction. She also told her that she has not smoked crack and has been clean for months. Mom reassured her that she loved her very much, and that she is now a new person with a new purpose. Mom told Jamie she hopes that one day all of her kids will be in the same room at the same time with her before she dies.

That's my wish as well.

Chapter 12
Road to Love— Through Love

My story would not be complete without discussing the ladies that played an important role in my life. Growing up, I did my best to figure out what love was. While my parents were hardly a typical couple, they did demonstrate for me in many positive ways what love between a man and a woman was. Many of my friends and relatives were in stable, long-term relationships. Early on I knew that's what I wanted in life—a wife who would love and cherish me, someone to raise a family with, someone to love until death do us part.

Looking back, there was always a compass inside of me directing me toward a certain type of lady. Every girl I've been in a relationship with has been smart, attractive, confident, and motivated. I needed to be in a relationship with a lady who could challenge me to be a better person, who was humble but not passive, and who would allow me to be her man above all others.

It took patience, faith, and effort, but I definitely married a terrific woman. Rachel is my soul mate, and my life is happy and complete because of her love. Before God blessed me with my bride, I was fortunate enough to be in some great relationships with some wonderful women.

I met my first real girlfriend, Aja, when I was in the seventh grade, and she was in the sixth. Many would say I was too young to understand the concept of a relationship, but I would tell them that we are all born with the ability to love. In Aja's case, it was her intelligence that sparked my interest. After we were "officially" together, I felt a sense of companionship I had never known. Aja helped me to understand that we were not put on this planet to be alone. Because I was so young, I did not know how to be a boyfriend, and I am sure she was figuring out things as well. But we learned together, and the times we spent with each other were fun. I especially bonded with her mother, who to this day I call Mom. At some point our relationship ended, but our friendship flourished. She is still a great friend to this day.

A year or so after Aja and I ceased being a couple, I met a young lady named Marissa. One evening I decided to catch the train over to Union Station in St. Louis by myself. After getting off the train, I headed toward the entrance. There was a group of girls congregating outside, so I stopped and said hello. We talked for a bit, and I sort of naturally focused on Marissa. We hit it off from the start, and we exchanged phone numbers. To my surprise, her mother lived about five streets away from my house. After we got together, I spent a lot of time hanging out with Marissa (and her mom) there. However, our timing could not have been worse. I was starting my high school football career, and she was getting into volleyball. We just did not have the time necessary to build and sustain a romantic relationship.

Mea was my high school sweetheart. I had known her for years prior to high school, we took classes together in middle school, but it was not until my last year of high school that I began to see her differently—not just as another girl, but potentially my girl. She had a unique history that made her stand out to me. When we were juniors, she had her first child. Mea did not allow her circumstances to defeat her. Her perseverance and drive to succeed impressed me, and I marveled at the strength of her character. After having her child, she was promptly back in school and back on the cheerleading team. For a time, I did not say much to her and watched from a distance.

During our last year of high school, we once again took a class together, Ms. Packard's keyboarding class. I started to see her daily but this time, unlike in middle school, I was attracted to her. We would probably not have had the chance to be together if she had not told me that she was single. Up to that point, all the time I knew her, she was in a committed relationship. After she let me know that relationship was a thing of the past, our conversations began and we soon agreed that we should try to be a couple.

This relationship was different for me. I was older, and

I understood more about life. I also knew more about love. It did not take long before she had me hooked. We were like a typical scene from a movie—the football player and cheerleader. She watched me play every game, and I watched her do toe touches from the sideline. We went to our senior prom together.

When high school was ending, we were making college decisions. She picked McKendree College. Shortly thereafter, I received a football scholarship from McKendree. The stars had aligned, at least so we thought, and our match made in heaven was going to continue. We went to college as a couple.

During orientation week, we learned an interesting statistic—60% of McKendree students marry one another. We thought that this was sure to be our ending. I learned many things from Mea while we were together. Some lessons were easy, and others hard. It was the hard ones that ultimately led to the end of our relationship. I was very prideful and immature. I did not see it then, but in retrospect, I had over-glorified my escape from the brutal environment where I grew up. I thought I was unconquerable, and my ego showed in a negative way. We parted ways, and I stayed single for most of my college career, but at the end of my junior year things changed again.

At that time, I lived in campus housing. My resident assistant (room police) was a senior named Rachel Witcher. The African-American population on campus was sparse so most of us knew each other, and everyone knew Rachel. At first, our contact was limited to her visits to ensure that we were complying with the campus rules regarding housing. We never had classes together, so I mostly saw her in passing. My fraternity brother was dating her best friend. When he told me that she was single and was no longer with her longtime boyfriend, my mind began to consider the possibilities. I had been single for a while at that point, and I was not necessarily looking to be in a relationship. I figured I was going to law school and I would meet someone there.

One day I sparked up a discussion with her in the clubhouse. Our conversation was great, so I found myself repeating the routine of finding her to talk. Before I knew it, I was interested in far more than just conversation—I wanted to explore the possibility of being in a long-term relationship with her. I knew that would be tough. She was a highly sought-after young lady, and from our general conversations about relationships, it appeared that she did not want to be in one at the moment. She said that she was enjoying her freedom from attachment after recently calling it quits with a serious boyfriend.

But I was determined, so I put the ball in motion. The first thing I had to do was get some of her time. I asked her if we could get some food one night, and she agreed. Our first outing was to Applebee's. She made it clear that we would be paying for our own meals, or going Dutch. It was my first time hearing of such a thing—I was used to paying for meals with girls. I suppose she just wanted to make sure that I knew that she did not expect me to pay for her food.

We both enjoyed each other's company and agreed to go out again.

Our next date was to the Legacy in St. Louis, Missouri. On Friday nights, the Legacy features spoken word poetry performances. Only this time we were not alone; Rachel asked her best friend to meet us there. She wasn't sure about me yet. We had a great time and on the way home, we talked for a while. She said that she was starting to like me but still had reservations.

That was my signal to kick things into high gear. The end of the school year was rapidly approaching, and she was graduating. My window of opportunity was closing fast. I told her that I was interested in us being together as a couple. One night she sat me down and shared some intimate details about her life and her feelings toward me. She wanted to make sure that I was aware of what I was getting. When she spoke, I realized that I didn't know all I needed to yet about Rachel Witcher.

Rachel explained that she came from the same type of negative environment and broken home as I did. My mother was not present, and neither was her father. We shared the same thoughts and goals—we were both not looking for a short-term boyfriend or girlfriend, we were looking for soul mates and spouses. I left that night with a greater sense of who she really was, and I went home to write. I had been writing poetry and competing in slams for a few years at that point. By the end of the night, I expressed everything that I felt about her in a poem I titled, "Kryptonite."

Rachel and I have been together since I recited "Krytonite" to her. In law school, Rachel was my girlfriend, then my fiancée, then my wife. We were married July 2, 2010.

We already have so many wonderful memories, and we are creating new ones every day. We have traveled the country and various parts of the world hand-in-hand. For me, nothing we have done together compares to the nights and times she pushed me to be better or not to give up. Rachel consistently reminds me that my destiny is bigger than my tough days. She is everything that I need in a woman, but she's not perfect. In fact, it is our imperfections combined that makes our relationship perfect. The love we share is indestructible and truly God given.

In September 2012, our love was made flesh when Courtney Robin Logan was born. She is truly the greatest gift I have ever received on this Earth. I watch in amazement as my daughter grows up before my eyes. I feel so blessed to have the opportunity to leave a legacy of hope in this world through her. I am forever indebted to my wife for making it all possible. My wife and daughter are both God's jewels. The Lord has given me the distinct role of being their keeper. Every day I ask Him for the strength to do my best for my girls and to be worthy of their love.

CHAPTER 13
Taking the Legal Road

I took a year off between college and law school. Why? I applied to 17 law schools and was denied to all but one, St. Louis University School of Law. St. Louis University has a summer program, which conditionally accepts students that might be on the lower end of the tier in terms of grades and standardized test scores, but "show the high degree of personal motivation" necessary to succeed in law school. They were describing me to a tee. I wanted to go to law school, and I refused to be denied, so I accepted the offer for the summer program a year later. Through the summer program, I gained admission into law school, but they did not have a seat open for me until the following September.

During my one-year hiatus from school, I worked as an assistant manager at Walgreens and as a sales associate at Jared Galleria of Jewelry. While at Walgreens from July 2008 to March 2009, I gained my first experience supervising people. I managed a multi-million dollar store. This was the first major responsibility I was asked to handle and I did well; although I knew that it was only a temporary position for me.

In March 2009, I switched jobs and moved to Jared Galleria of Jewelry. I took a pay cut when I switched positions. At the time, Walgreens did not have slots for part-time assistant managers. I was gearing up for law school, which was right around the corner. I worked part-time at Jared during law school to help pay the bills. I actually started law school in May 2009 but did not formally enter the program until August.

Law school is designed for a specific type of person. For me, the work itself was challenging but not overwhelming. The hours can be onerous. I was used to working hard, which was not the case for a lot of my fellow students. I had been in the work force working full-time and then some for a year plus, so law school was actually a delight. I knew what it was like to stock shelves, deal with customers and employees, and stack 30 cases of water all in the middle of the night. Thanks to my experiences at McKendree, I was well prepared for law school and was not coming in a step behind like I did to college.

I had a couple of key mentors in law school. As a first-year student, I met Sheena Hamilton, an African-American woman and a third-year law student. She approached me and gave me the "lay of the land." The first year of law school is very competitive. Everyone is vying for the top spots because the best jobs generally go to the top students.

Sheena expressed to me the importance of doing great work, but also staying vigilant at the same time. Whether I wanted to believe it or not, there were many people that didn't want me to outperform them. After Sheena graduated, she came back to coach my National Championship Moot Court team. She remains a close friend to this day and consistently offers me sound advice.

Oliver Beatty was another law school rock star that took me under his wing. He was a year ahead of me. Oliver was the type of person that was very exclusive and getting into his inner circle was tough. But he was the son of a gravedigger and grew up in Gary, Indiana, so the common elements of our backgrounds made us click. He helped shape my legal career.

After competitively debating for almost my entire undergraduate career, I needed something to fill that void in law school. Moot court was the answer. Moot court is a law school extracurricular activity in which students take part in a simulated appellate argument. Students write a legal brief on the legal issue given, and argue their case in front of a panel of judges. During my first year of law school, I competed in my first moot court competition. My transition from debate to moot court was tough. Debate is a very adversarial process, but moot court is more conversational. My first-year results reflected this transition. My partner and I were quarter-finalist in our competition. While some would be proud of such an accomplishment, I knew that I could do better, and after that competition, I vowed to the director of the national tournament in a private discussion that I would be back in 2011 and win the national title. I did, with my partner, Kirsten Staples, and coach, Sheena Hamilton.

One day in my second year of law school, I was summoned to the career services office at the law school and told that the United States Attorney for the Southern District of Illinois, Steve Wigginton, wanted to meet me. So, I contacted his office and set it up. When I went to his office, he told me that he saw an article in the newspaper about my moot court victory and that I was from East St. Louis. He explained that he was born in East St. Louis, and the city had a special place in his heart. He presented me with a laminated, signed copy of the newspaper article. I was humbled and honored. During my last year of law school, I had the distinct pleasure of working for his office as a clerk. It was then that Steve introduced me to Brendan Kelly, the State's Attorney for St. Clair County, who would one day be my boss.

After my first year of law school, I worked for Land of Lincoln, which is a legal aid group that serves underprivileged populations. It is located in East St. Louis. Here I had the opportunity to see a different side of the law. I began to understand how powerful my craft was and how much personal responsibility I had to become a good, ethical lawyer. Our office was our clients' only opportunity for legal recourse, their last line of defense. We were like the public defender in the civil world.

During my second year, I worked for a defense law firm which is located in Edwardsville, Illinois, as a summer associate. I learned a great deal about the law, and acquired valuable tools for becoming a practicing attorney. The work was complex and intriguing. I was forced to think outside the box to solve the issues confronting me. A few weeks after my summer internship was completed, I was offered a full-time job after graduation, which I accepted.

To my utter amazement, in August before my third year started, I already had my first job locked down. I was greatly relieved because the economy at the time was still mired in recession. I clerked for Federal District Court Judge Carol Jackson in the Eastern District of Missouri during the fall of my third year and worked for the United States Attorney during my last spring in law school.

Steve Wigginton understood that I wanted to be a trial lawyer. To accomplish this goal, I needed courtroom experience. He impressed upon me that the best way to do that was to become a prosecutor. Brendan Kelly would come to the United States Attorney's office for meetings regularly, while I worked there during the spring of 2012. At some point, I sent him my résumé, and he scheduled an interview with me.

When I went to Brendan's office to meet with him, he had just left on an urgent call. He assigned his First Assistant State's Attorney, James Piper, to speak with me. I remember that James took me to lunch at a Greek restaurant where we had gyros. He explained the direction the office was headed under the helm of Brendan and the value I could add to the office. East St. Louis is located in St. Clair County, so many of the battles they were plagued with came from my city. They sold me on their dream of making my community a better place. I was convinced that I could help them in this effort because I had lived in the community that they were so desperately trying to save. More importantly, at that lunch it was revealed that Jim Piper, the man sitting across the table, was one of the prosecutors that tried my brother's case. That lunch altered my career.

I called the law firm I was initially going to work for and told them that I was going to go work for Brendan Kelly. It was a tough call to make. All my life I had been working hard to gain a comfortable lifestyle. I was tired of struggling, but there was a greater agenda to be served at the time. I was taking a pay cut in the hope that I could make a difference.

It was the best decision I ever made. It was in line with my choice to lay down my football helmet. I truly loved being a prosecutor. Because of my life experiences, I was able to discern things about people and cases my colleagues often missed. More importantly, I was in the courtroom daily. I had the opportunity to appear frequently in hearings and to try jury trials.

When I started the job working on behalf of the State of Illinois, my wife, Rachel, was eight months pregnant. Rachel and I got engaged after my first year of law school. We were married the summer before my second year of law school. In my third year of law school, she got pregnant.

After we had the baby, Rachel was a stay-at-home mom.

Unfortunately, with all the financial pressures mounting, I was placed in a position where I needed more money to sustain my household. The combination of having a brand-new baby, Rachel not working, all the bills that were piling up—student loans, baby expenses, rent payments—I had to get a job in the corporate law arena.

I reached out to the law firm where I interned, and they were very receptive to the idea of me coming back to work for them. So in February 2013, I finished my full-time work with the state and went to work as an associate at the firm. After some discussion with both parties, we agreed that I would be able to work in the capacity of a Special Assistant State's Attorney on a pro bono basis. Which would allow me to help with social programs that would positively affect East St. Louis and the surrounding communities. While I miss being a full-time prosecutor, I'm learning the ropes of the corporate law world.

But I have not forgotten about East St. Louis. I am still working to make a difference in my community. Even though I'm still young and on the way up in this world, I have a few ideas . . .

CHAPTER 14
CREATIVE POLICY

As a society, we can do more to help kids make better choices before they become teens and young adults. I took full advantage of all of these types of programs, and it helped me. Smokey did as well. Growing up in the type of environment I did, it was important to stay busy with positive things. Negativity was everywhere. In this chapter, I want to talk about some of the key things that allowed me to escape poverty and the inner city. The one thing that truly got me on the path to my current and growing success, and what children of the inner city need more than anything—is a solid education. Also, there is a desperate need for community involvement. It takes a village to raise a child. This could not be truer in my case.

I am a living example that various social development strategies can lead to healthier behaviors for kids growing up in harsh environments. All kids deserve opportunities, recognition, and the chance to develop their skills. The problem comes when these opportunities are lacking, and it increases risk factors that can be detrimental to a child's growth and development. The whole point is to increase these kids' protective factors and eliminate, or at least greatly reduce, risk factors.

Conditions that are prevalent in communities like where I grew up, such as poverty, discrimination, unemployment, lack of education, poor health, and utter despair, set the scene for drug and alcohol-related problems. It goes without saying that we need to do all we can to alleviate these dreadful conditions. More importantly, if we ever hope to see the cycle of poverty eradicated, we must take proactive steps to ensure this is so.

The risk factors clearly include the domains of family, school, peers, individuals, and the community at large. And while it is of the utmost importance that we work to enhance the abilities and skills of individual kids, it's just as important that we concentrate on evolving and improving our social systems to create more favorable conditions. Our problem is intertwined. So, taking a traditional approach to a novel problem would be a waste of time. Policy makers need to think outside the box when considering an inner city program effectiveness before its implementation. Also, we have to find ways to increase the number of inner city children who grow up and become productive members of society. Where do we start?

We must start with parental involvement. It is without question that a child's home life affects his or her ability to learn. Children need a support system when the school day ends. However, in the inner city the family structure is shattered. Unfortunately, many inner city parents lack education or they are apathetic to whether the child gets optimal value out of their education. This is the reality we face. In fact, this is a contributing factor to why the truancy rate is so high; parents do not take an affirmative role in ensuring that their child is participating in the educational experience. Many kids in the inner city attend on an irregular basis. If they are not in school, they are not able to build a solid foundation of academic skills—even at the most basic level. These youths have neither dropped out of school officially nor are they exactly on long leave due to an illness. So they're truants. They're at risk of dropping out of school altogether and way too young, and never getting the skills needed to become contributing members to their society and community. Parents play a vital role in ensuring that their children are engaged and attending school. Some parents just turn a blind eye to the issue. As I said previously, it was my home life that pushed me more toward school, but for many students, it is the opposite. There are high school students who are working to support their families. It is important that we have adequate resources to offset this.

We need parents to care about their child's education. It has been shown that parents who demonstrate care and love for their kids, and are more involved in their activities and interests and monitor their behaviors, in turn provide more stability for that child. This should be a highlight in our educational system. My mother and father were so busy battling their addictions that school became a solo venture on my part. When I turned 16, my father told me that he would not make me go to school anymore, and that if I went, it was because I wanted to be there. That was a lot of responsibility to put on a child. However, I loved school, so this did not affect my thirst to be in a classroom. But give that option to a person that loathes school, and they will become the next high school dropout. We must find ways, to the extent that we can, to ensure that a child's home life is not completely counterbalancing the work the teachers and administrators are performing on a daily basis in the schools.

Teachers are pivotal in our war on poverty in the inner city. Once we get a child to school they have to want to stay, and this is where I believe the teachers play a key role. Believe it or not, passion is still important in educating students. We need to ensure that our educators are fresh and excited to deliver an education. As a student, I fed off of my teachers' enthusiasm when they taught me. The inverse was true as well. Classrooms where I saw and knew the teacher was a "paycheck collector" stifled my education. Teachers that genuinely care about their learners and strive to demonstrate concern for a child's academic and social growth help to build a positive environment and successful development.

Teachers that work in the inner city have to serve as a "beacon of hope" for their students. In many instances, the odds are against many of these students, and so many have already given up on them. I was one of them, and so were my friends. However, all it took was a teacher to continuously brainwash me into thinking I was better than my surroundings. Teachers are building blocks of dynamic futures. However, some teachers devastate destinies instead. Too many times the administration allows teachers to stay in these positions long after they have lost the desire to actually teach. This is problematic, and there is no room for these types of educators. This simply cannot happen. The students already are up against the tide, and these types of educators only widen the education gap in the inner city compared to affluent school districts. I'll admit working in these school districts is no easy feat. It is critical that the teachers we employ are locked in the mission of educating by any means necessary and think outside the box. I had those teachers. They were successful.

We also need creativity back in the classrooms. Art and cultural programs for inner city students can help. It's already been proven that such programs work well to keep kids off the dangerous streets. When I was in middle school, I participated in a Sim City competition that my art teacher pitched to me. We designed a model city on the computer and had to build a model of the city using ceramics. We presented our design at the St. Louis Science Center among students from all over Missouri and Illinois. It was an amazing experience. This encouraged growth and developed my creative potential. Now, I have birthed a book. Without creativity, we tend to become careful, cautious, and fearful of changes. Through art, though, a student can let go of their fears and prepare to take healthy risks. Programs like these don't need to set out to train budding artists. The whole idea is to get creative with problem solving and get the kids to understand that they really can do anything as far as the eye can see.

Creative outlets are a great source of education, anger management, and self-esteem building. Kids could play musical instruments, paint, and even do artistic things such as creating ceramics. In fact, kids in cities that have already put such programs in place have been shown to score better marks in science, math, and foreign languages because they're partaking in activities that make them better learners. Creative outlets also help to enhance emotional well-being. These types of programs really help to expand focus and awareness since activities like art and music demand concentration. However, based on "budgetary restrictions" many of these programs have been eliminated. This has taken major tools away from our educators in their fight to educate our nation's next generation. Schools have taken a robotic, assembly-line approach toward education. In doing so, they have stripped teachers' ability to tap into the essence of a student, and the ability to find out what interests them other than math and science.

Students are suffering educationally from large class sizes, too. My class sizes were between 30 and 35 from middle school through high school. It is very hard to get a good education when there are so many students vying for the teacher's attention. Then when you add disturbances into the equation, it is almost impossible at times. There are just typically so many people that a teacher is able to help. In an interview, Jonathan Kozol, author of Savage Inequalities, talked directly to this point. He stated when he is posed the question, "Does class size really matter?" by his affluent friends he simply states, "It works for your kids, doesn't it?" To which he typically doesn't get a reply. The truth is reducing class size is very imperative in a student getting the maximum educational value out of school. In fact, many colleges and universities use this as an advertising tool to attract students to come and pay the tuition. It is obvious that class size matters and there is value attached to it.

However, until class sizes can be reduced dramatically we have to find ways to effectively reach students there in the classes with 30 and 35 students. I suggest the small group method. This would let students work through issues and learn in a collaborative way, but also would give the teacher an opportunity to better address concerns when meeting with each individual group. Of course the teacher would have to be available more often to those who are have a tough time grasping the material, but it generally would free the teacher up to teach the entire class. This at least would give the classroom better structure. The small group method was very effective when I entered undergraduate education, and if applied to inner city high schools it could have the same effect. However, the optimal learning environment is in a small class setting.

The biggest black eye the school system currently has—its inadequate social services. Social services are critical in such brutal, impoverished environments. We need increased social services programs. It is sad I did not know my school had a social worker. Furthermore, to make it worse, the social worker we did have was only for students that had special education services. Here I was in honors classes reliving hell every day, and I did not have access to a social worker. If I had been offered the help I so desperately needed when I was younger, I would have been able to cope better, which would have allowed me to learn on a higher level. I had many unresolved issues, and sadly, in comparison to others, my issues were small. The most frustrating thing is that social services are typically the first on the chopping block when it comes to budget allocation. We are doing our children a huge disservice by not giving them the help that they need. In the same vein, we ask them to perform on a high level on standardized testing. Children need effective ways to deal with the chaos where they are forced to live. This investment will allow a student to be more attentive, productive, and alert, which would enable them to gain a quality education

However, in the world we currently live in this is not the case. Children are being asked to juggle all of their hardships, issues, and problems while at the same time excel in school. This is ludicrous and almost impossible. We are building a bridge of air and asking our children to walk across it blindfolded. Student cannot get an optimal education without the adequate help that they need. In no way am I saying we can stop all the negative things that happen in a child's life away from school, but what I am saying is that we must effectively control the aspects we do have power over, such as social services. The school house was my safe haven and is for thousands of kids across this country. We must be proactive and not reactive. Waiting until a child is being disruptive or abusive and then expelling them is not the answer. We need to find ways to dig deeper and help solve the actual issue if we are to be successful in educating the next generation of inner city youth.

Year-round schooling is the answer to solving the educational gap in the inner city. As in my case, many times going home can be a child's worst nightmare. We can combat this by shielding children from their harsh environment by immersing them in educational activities and opportunities. This would also make education readily accessible and widely available. There is no doubt that education is the key to breaking out of the inner city. Education and training also can break poverty's back because it is cyclical. This would also give students another alternative other than being on the streets for 90 days in the summer. While there are breaks in the year-round schooling model, which are typically 3–6 weeks, it is not 90 days in a row unsupervised on the streets. It is important we monopolize students' time with positive things. The more time they have to be on the streets, the more time they have to fall victim to all of the negative activity around them. I think this is the single most effective thing we can do in the inner city to curb crime and increase the success among our youth.

The youth is our way forward. Poverty is a mindset. Thus, we must educate our way out of it. The more educational exposure that we give our youth, the more education becomes desirable. The year-round schooling concept solves a lot of issues in the inner-city. It allows students to become more connected to the school environment, structure, and discipline. Furthermore, it allows students to build a stronger and deeper bond with the teachers. I believe throughout time this could go a long way to curb the negative impacts the environment has on the students' lives. This is because students would spend more time in the school environment, under the care of educated teachers; more than they would in the streets and in negative environments at home.

Some people may ask the question "Who is actually raising the children?" There are people who believe educators' only job is to teach. However, my most effective teachers growing up had an all-encompassing view of what the educational model should look like. They had a great role in raising me by reinforcing good habits and refusing to accept subpar behavior or work. This was not the traditional model of teaching. If they had not employed different strategies to teach me, I might be behind bars or in a grave. So either we invest in education for youth or we build more prisons and dig more graves. However you decide to look at it, the money will be spent. Why not invest in breaking the cycle of poverty?

Until inner city school districts implement year-round schooling, we need to increase summer enrichment programs. These are typically courses and programs offered in the summertime that covers specific educational topics. There is typically a summer lunch program connected to these programs as well, which is important because a lot of students rely on school meals to make it through the day. So, when the regular school year ends, the breakfast and lunch they received daily disappears. My first summer enrichment program was when I was in second grade. It was at a local college. For two summers in a row, I spent time building model robots and rockets. I could have spent those hours in the streets. The summer before my freshman year of high school, I was in the summer enrichment program at East St. Louis Senior High School. The class was about water quality. We spent the whole summer talking about how to determine whether water was quality or not. This summer culminated with a trip to the water plant where we were able to see the entire process of how water is purified.

There are other programs that I found very effective. All through my primary education, I can recall being a part of some type of after-school program. These programs served as a way to extend the school day for me. For me, it really wasn't about the activities on a certain day, but it was an opportunity in a safe place away from home. Also, they provided another meal. The by-product was increased learning opportunities to have more life exposure and make new friends. The key word here—safe haven. We need more family centers and schools in the city to offer safe places for children where they can occupy their time on the weekends and after school. For me, it was very valuable.

These programs brought in a variety of strategies and programs such as conflict resolution. This is very important growing up in a hostile environment. The ability to come up with creative ways to solve problems, such as allowing for involved parties to express their point of view and voice their interests, can go a long way to finding solutions that will be acceptable to both parties. These programs identified that while conflict is natural, we needed to learn skills to deal with conflict in nonviolent ways. These programs were comprehensive and encompassed several components such as anger control, moral reasoning, social skills, and collaborative ways to solve problems. They also provided cultural, educational, and recreational activities that were overseen by trained staff and offered me an opportunity for community service. For me, the opportunities to serve others helped me build my sense of self-worth and self-value.

I can't stress this enough. Education is key. Knowledge is power. We should not be afraid to try creative solutions to our inner city problems either.

Kids in the inner city usually don't have the wherewithal to enjoy the opportunities enjoyed by other people. And everyone in the city is affected—from elderly couples to families and young working residents. But it's the kids that are affected the most.

These kids aren't afforded adequate facilities to grow up

healthy, educated, and ready to climb corporate ladders. The parks are derelict, and the education is pitifully poor. And for most kids, the chance at a solid education is often their only chance of getting off the streets and out of the city. But if they're not given those opportunities and the same sort of education as other kids, they'll never get out and the problem continues to grow.

Learning at schools needs to be of the caliber that it is extended beyond the classroom walls. There should be programs that allow the kids to learn other essential life skills such as working in groups to achieve common goals. We should not just be teaching kids math or reading concepts without teaching life skills as well.

We have to have programs that set out to help these kids achieve more than they're allowed in a mainstream inner city school environment. Programs that can reach out to self-motivated students who want academic assistance, those who want to get into a good high school, and those who want to get into a good college. These types of programs bring summer school into play. But it needs to start with the teachers. These programs need to recruit experienced, patient, and motivated individuals—be they college students, high school students, or actual educators. These have to be selfless people, driven to share a love of learning. Whoever they are, they need to be volunteers geared toward drawing kids into the classroom for self-improvement.

Students should want to get closer and build up lasting friendships with each other and the teachers. They should feel safe enough to chat with teachers about their lives, school, in fact anything significant going on with them. The personal relationships between teachers and kids are just as beneficial as the learning process. In effect, these teachers are mentors.

Kids need to be educated on the world outside the walls of their communities. I saved the best for last. As a young child, this allowed me to shape my perception of what my future was to be. It has been shown that the earlier a child is put on a college campus, the more likely they are to enroll in college. I was in second grade when I was on a college campus for the first time. I grew to understand that my environment where I lived was not the way that the rest of the world was. By the time I got to high school, my dreams soared. Many nights I would find myself in my car driving through subdivisions in affluent neighborhoods picking out which house I would buy when I got older.

Many kids growing up in these environments believe that what they see every day is the best life that they can have. They believe that successful people live in the beautiful subdivisions that are reserved for those that don't look like them. It is important that we reach children at an early age and show them the bigger world that exists outside of places such as East St. Louis. There are programs in East St. Louis that do a good job of this already. Some of them are the New Yu Youth Movement, Christian Activity Center, Jackie Joyner-Kersee Center, Upward Bound, and the East St. Louis Dream Center. There are others and this is to just name a few. There are churches that have great initiatives in this area too.

Finally, and most importantly, before the policy maker, school teacher, or school administration can have a serious discussion about these issues, they all have to agree on the fact that children's lives in the inner city are "different." I am different, and the way I learn and grasp concepts even now as a practicing attorney is different. Thus, the way we approach the educational model must be fine-tuned to the realities that are facing our students. However, if we do not accept that fact, we are doomed to fail. Our educational strategies will never be focused enough to reach the student populace. Some will squeeze their way through just as I did. The primary role of our educational system is to ensure that students have the best education possible, and without the necessary resources it is impossible. Even now in 2014, most children are left to their own whims. I did not have this type of help, and I was forced to either sink or swim all alone. Luckily, I figured out a way to float. Sadly, many drown waiting on a life preserver. The system has to be that life preserver.

Many will say that this is unfair because we should not be diverting our resources to just one populated area. I believe the only fairness issue lies in us not sending those resources. There is so much opportunity and access in schools outside the inner city. It is my belief that just because you were born poor does not mean you should be subjected to a substandard education. I think many of our people would agree with this supposition. However, when it's time to actually increase funding, then it becomes an issue. I've always considered myself a smart person, however, I failed math and English my first semester of my undergraduate study. My inadequate primary education will follow me for the rest of my life. I was not able to qualify for scholarships because I didn't have a strong GPA. Thus, I had to pay a portion of my undergraduate education through loan money. Furthermore, since I had a bad freshman year of undergrad, my GPA tanked and made my applications to law school weaker. Therefore, I had to pay for law school out of my pocket. So there is no denying the fact that a primary education can haunt a person for the rest of their lives, or it could be the best thing that ever happened to them. So, even for a person like me that makes it out of the inner city, I am still haunted by a subpar primary education. This cycle is repeated too often.

CHAPTER 15
A NEW DIRECTION

During my short lifetime, I have been witness to great social change. When I was a preschooler, communism in Eastern Europe collapsed and the Cold War ended. While I was in grade school, apartheid in South Africa was dismantled and a new multi-racial democracy was born. The year I graduated from college, an African-American man was elected President of the United States.

So when I hear people and politicians say things such as, "Nothing good can come from East St. Louis" or "East St. Louis is cursed" or "We can't improve East St. Louis," I get upset. I know that East St. Louis can, and eventually will, become a better place to live and raise a family. With God's help, positive change is very possible.

In order for change to take root and blossom, the widely held perception that East St. Louis is a hopeless cause must be effectively challenged. How can we accomplish this goal? This book is one step in that direction. More current and former East St. Louis citizens need to step forward and tell their stories of success and triumph over obstacles. Just as I did when I was in college, when confronted with negative stereotypes about our community we need to step up and say, "Wait a minute. Learn the facts before you judge our city. There are things we can do to make things better."

There must be more financial and political accountability. It would serve no purpose for me to detail in these pages the seemingly endless list of scandals involving public officials in East St. Louis. What is required is this—those elected to public office must become more responsible and dedicated to the best interests of the public. As voters, we must demand integrity from our political leaders above all else.

How will perceptions change? The first and most important step in that direction is a switch at the top. Political figures, from the Mayor to the City Council to the Chief of Police, must be beyond reproach. It is well past time that men and women of the highest caliber stepped up to fill these vital roles in our community.

The collapsing infrastructure of East St. Louis must also be addressed. My community cannot move forward without adequate housing, sewers, roads, bridges, and utility services. Our local political leadership must work with state and federal authorities to address this problem, which long ago reached the crisis stage.

Why have we not seen more attention paid to East St. Louis from the national media? In 2012, St. Louis television station KMOV aired a multi-part series on East St. Louis called "America's War Zone." In great detail, KMOV reporters explored the political corruption and neglect, the rampant crime, devastated infrastructure, and depressed local economy of my city. Right here, smack dab in the middle of our prosperous country, is a not-so-tiny enclave with a homicide rate 20 times the national average and twice the rate of Gary, Indiana; Detroit, Michigan, and St. Louis, Missouri.

The murder rate in East St. Louis is even higher than the murder rate per capita in Iraq, according to a 2012 interview with my friend United States Attorney Steve Wigginton for an editorial at http://www.stltoday.com.

Where is CNN? Where is Fox News? Where are CBS, NBC, and ABC? East St. Louis is a national tragedy, yet few outside the local area seem to care. Why? I wish I knew. Public awareness and action is very important in breaking the shackles of poverty. When I describe for people outside of southern Illinois what it's like to live in East St. Louis, they are appalled. "Why doesn't somebody do something?" they ask. "Why don't more people in America know about this problem?" they wonder.

People need to care again. As a nation, we are all diminished by the fact that places like East St. Louis still exist. To some extent, we all bear a bit of responsibility for neglecting our brothers and sisters who are trapped in this endless cycle of crime and poverty. With sufficient social and political will, we can transform the city I love from a hellhole to the wonderful city on the river that it once was.

Just as young black men have a choice, so do we, the American public. If as a society we care enough about the oppressed overseas to send thousands of troops and spend billions of dollars to help them, if we care enough to build more and more prisons to warehouse an endless stream of new felons, and if we care enough to spend billions of dollars to rescue Wall Street banks and brokerage firms from the consequences of their own greed, can't we find the resources necessary to help the good people of East St. Louis help themselves?

As a prosecutor and the brother of one deceased and one living ex-felon, I assure you that putting more people in prison is not the answer to East St. Louis' crime problem. Individuals should be held accountable for their actions; I am a strong believer in personal responsibility. What I am saying is the same thing Steve Wigginton said in that interview, "We can't arrest and prosecute our way out of this."

Young black men growing up in East St. Louis need jobs. *Employment is the best way to combat crime.* I gained a sense of self-respect, of accomplishment and of achievement through both my academic and employment experiences as a youngster. We need to make an effort, perhaps a herculean effort, to bring employment opportunities back to East St. Louis. This can be done in many ways, and I'm not trying to beat the drum for any one of them, *I'm beating it for all* of them—tax incentives, business incentives, public employment, charitable foundations, etc. All good ideas should be put on the table and fully explored.

When I read dry statistics about the costs of incarcerating men, I often shake my head in both wonder and disgust. Depending on where you're housing a person, the number is between $30,000 and $40,000 per year to keep a man behind bars. Pick whichever number you like, the figure will still be *vastly understated.* You must add to these costs the care and support of the family and children left behind when the man goes to prison, the lost revenues in economic activity and taxes from his absence from the work force, the economic impact on the community of the crimes he commits, and on and on.

The almost wholesale incarceration of a large segment of our community is part of the problem, not the solution.

But how do we stop this vicious cycle?

In the first chapter, I promised you that I would tell you the truth, and that the truth will set you free. Now is the time for some hard truth.

Young black men need to step up and take responsibility for their own lives. All too often they take the easy way out by slinging dope and committing property crimes. Why? Because their fathers were absent from their lives or, worse, they were setting a bad example for them by engaging in criminal activities themselves.

I have a message for my young black brothers—quit blaming the world, or your circumstances, or "white people" or injustice or whatever and take control of your own life. You are not a victim! We are all dealt certain cards to play with. We do not get to pick those cards, that is not how life works. Figure out a way to win with what you've got.

I have great empathy for our young black men growing up in oppressive circumstances. As I have detailed in this book, I know how tough it is to be born and raised in East St. Louis. I want to do everything in my power to help them succeed—that's why I speak to them regularly and volunteer my time to make a difference.

But all the empathy in the world cannot change reality— your decisions determine your destiny.

If you live in East St. Louis or Gary, Indiana, or on the south side of Chicago or in Detroit, and you're black, you must take advantage of whatever opportunities are available to you. Do not wait for things to come to you. In some instances, you will have to make your own opportunities.

I believe in the power of one person. We can choose to help each other, to have children in a responsible manner, and to work for a living and not to steal or sell poison to our brothers and sisters.

We can become the bright, shining stars God intended us to be.

I chose that path and I encourage others to follow me.

References

1. Savage Inequalities, Children in America's Schools, Jonathan Kozol, 1991. A finalist for the 1992 National Book Critics Circle Award and awarded the New England Book Award. Reprint ISBN 0-06-097499-0.

2. GreatSchools website, http://www.greatschools.org/.

3. Editorial Board, The Platform, "Editorial: East St. Louis as 'America's war zone'," May 6, 2012, http://www.stltoday.com/news/opinion/columns/the-platform/editorial-east-st-louis-as-america-s-war-zone/article_bbabd2f7-18a5-5c5b-82c6-3ab23b08cc08.html, Retrieved January 10, 2013.

About the Author

Courtney R. Logan, Esq. is a sought-after keynote speaker and author. While not speaking and writing, he spends his time mentoring and motivating youth to make wise choices. He is on an international mission to save youth by empowering them with his message of hope. He is a practicing attorney and serves as an assistant adjunct professor at his alma mater Saint Louis University School of Law. You can find him on Twitter at @courtneyrlogan and his home page is www.courtneyrlogan.com. This is his first book.

#shapedbyfire

How to Help This Book

I believe in the power of one person. You have the ability to help me spread this message to the rest of world. This vision depends in large part on my reputation, coupled with referrals and recommendations from people like you. Collectively, these will allow me to make an everlasting impact on the world.

You can help this book by doing one or more of the following:

- Review the book on amazon.com, bn.com, goodreads.com, or other related sites. The more honest, the better.
- Mention the book on your blog, Facebook, Twitter, Reddit, Google+, LinkedIn, Pinterest, and other sites you frequent.
- Recommend the book to family members, colleagues, your boss, friends, and people who might find it interesting.
- Give as a gift.
- If you know people who work in newspapers, magazines, television, or industry groups, I'd love a referral or reference. Social media has not entirely replaced the

importance of traditional media.
- Visit www.courtneyrlogan.com and read, watch, and listen to your heart's content.

I do not expect to get rich by writing books. I wrote this book to save lives and enhance futures. I believe that I have something meaningful to say, and by sharing others will be encouraged to do the same. I feel a sense of satisfaction from creating a physical product from scratch. Also, I believe that this book will make other good things happen for me and others. At the same time, though, producing a quality text takes an enormous amount of time, effort, and money. Every additional copy sold helps make the next book possible.

Thanks again.

— Courtney

www.ingramcontent.com/pod-product-compliance
Lightning Source LLC
Chambersburg PA
CBHW032040290426
44110CB00012B/889